Idle

Chris Roberts was born in London since 1982. He has written about music, films and books for a wide range of publications, and was staff writer at *Melody Maker* from 1987 to 1991. In 1992 he released two highly acclaimed EPs with the band Catwalk and since then has been working on the debut Sclalaland album, *Breathing Down the Neck of Meaning*. He was recently appointed Deputy Editor at *Ikon* magazine.

IDLE WORSHIP

HOW POP EMPOWERS THE WEAK, REWARDS THE FAITHFUL AND SUCCOURS THE NEEDY

Edited by
Chris Roberts

HarperCollins*Publishers*

HarperCollins*Publishers*
77–85 Fulham Palace Road,
Hammersmith, London W6 8JB

A Paperback Original 1994
1 3 5 7 9 8 6 4 2

A catalogue record for this book
is available from the British Library

ISBN 0 00 638266 5

Set in Linotron Caledonia by
Rowland Phototypesetting Ltd
Bury St Edmunds, Suffolk

Printed in Great Britain by
HarperCollinsManufacturing Glasgow

:|| Contents

:|| Illustrations

:|| Introduction

So I'VE JUST GOT UP THE STAIRS with my piping hot
fish and chips and the phone's ringing. I put my fish and chips
on top of the stove, which hasn't worked for eighteen months,
and think: this better be quick. 'Yeah?' I snarl with all the
hostility I can muster.

'Hello, Chris?'

'Yeah.' (A sort of three-quarters snarl, jockeying for
position.)

'Hi, it's Bono here.'

I *don't* say: Bono *Who*?? Neither do I ask him to ring back
after I've had my chips. I switch into what I consider to be
sweetness-and-light mode and thank him for phoning, and we
talk about Frank Sinatra. 'Have you got five minutes? I'll read
it out to you,' he says. Oh, I think so. The chips can go hang.
Because no matter how jaded you are by working around the
music industry, or for that matter how jaded you are by Life
Itself (big themes! already! yeah!), when one of the world's
most famous rock stars phones you up it is still, frankly, quite
exciting. It is more exciting than chips, say.

The absurdity of the situation does not escape me; neither
does the thought that he'd be perfectly within his rights to ⪼

have a moan about one or two of my U2 reviews over the years. Yet he seems to want to talk about his enthusiasm for Frank, and stress the point that however many fans you're perceived to have acquired yourself, you don't stop *being* one, it doesn't go away, you can still be *starstruck*.

While some of the contributors to *Idle Worship* remain rather *gloriously* starstruck, others remember when they *were*, with affection or disbelief. Some admit to hideous embarrassment, while others eulogise the inspiration and motivation drawn from leading pop lights. Others go off on berserk 'irrelevant' tangents, which is fine by me.

Some time ago I was approached by Philip Gwyn Jones at HarperCollins with a view to compiling a book that ran against the grain of 'hagiographical, pompous, inane' writing on modern music. I was very impressed by the word 'hagiographical', and, after looking it up, and demanding a rider of Last-Days-of-Pompeii proportions, set myself to the task. This involved innumerable letters and phone calls and becoming The Nag from Hell. Then saying, 'Yeah, whatever. Sounds good to me,' whenever a writer or musician got out of bed long enough to call me back and proffer a synopsis. We wanted an eclectic mix of story-tellers and I think I can safely say the diversity herein, by accident or design, is both luscious and arousing. Many PRs were very helpful over the course of this book's protracted birth. And some were entirely bloody useless. Thanks to the former.

Perhaps unsurprisingly, it was the more established 'writers' who delivered the goods most promptly, increasing the literary merit of my letterbox before I could say Smokey Robinson. I am baffled as to how they found the time when they should be doing proper joiny-up writing, but hey, in the world of rock'n'roll there's no sleep till the typewriter ribbon gets all snaggled. *Dreams of Sex and Stagediving* author Martin Millar compares and contrasts his experiences attending noisy hairy gigs seventeen years apart, discovering in the process that the Pixies pummel the sweat glands as ferociously as Led Zeppelin fired the awe. After sending me this he rang to see if I could get him on the guest list for Smashing Pumpkins, which proves his reborn zeal knows no bounds. *Fever Pitch* author Nick Hornby's secret admiration for the very great Rod Stewart is long overdue for exposure, especially since he once made a veiled reference in a popular magazine to my owning a Genesis album. Still, no-one twigged except me. Any jibes about the Johnny Cougar debut album will however be matched by a ruthless description of the neo-Rod haircut sported in his days as midfield dynamo for the college Third XI. Ah, the joys of the old school tie set-up. When I first discussed this book with *Desperadoes* author Joseph O'Connor, whose sister is no stranger to the slings and arrows of pop fortune, I was myopic enough to mumble, 'Hmm, I don't know if Bob Geldof's very topical.' Reading his masterful evocation of a troubled Dublin childhood and adolescence amid a traumatised family I can only humbly admire his sangfroid.

Then strange things arrived from the land that God is asked to bless rather frequently. The golden words of Stephen J. Malkmus, of the intriguing Californian band Pavement, narrate a futuristic fantasy wherein Eddie Vedder of Pearl Jam is a visionary monk, while lampooning most living artists in any medium. Thurston Moore of Sonic Youth gives us a thoroughly uplifting tale of sex and drugs (and possibly some rock'n'roll too) in New York City. 'It's fiction,' he informs me. 'I suspect you may have to censor the "dirty" language by using asterisks but hopefully this won't be the case.' The first time I read this frank take on *Breakfast at Tiffany's* filtered through Charles Bukowski, I thought: shame we can't use it. Then good taste prevailed. The lyrics that close the story come from the *Experimental Jet-Set, Trash and No Star* LP. Kristin Hersh of Boston's Throwing Muses recalls how a chronic fear of her father's Patti Smith records gave way to a fascination with armpits and fingers . . .

Caitlin Moran has been described as 'precocious' more times than she's been described as 'an orgasm octopus', allegedly. The presenter of Channel 4's 'Naked City' testifies to the quivering, jutting, throbbing joys of Suede, as so many young people today are wont to do. What with comedy being the new rock'n'roll (at least at the time of writing, 11.56pm), Robert Newman's teenage recollection of a chance meeting with the mothers of proto-punk band Crass works on about nine levels, by my reckoning. Cosmic link: the first words Robert ever spoke to me (come to think of it, the only words he's ever spoken to me) were: 'You get mentioned in *Fever Pitch*, don't you?' See, it's all coming together. Which is exactly what I thought when the final part of a serial rant from the inimitable Mark E. Smith of evergreen Manchester mavericks The Fall reached my filing cabinet, the afore-mentioned dysfunctional stove.

The side-splitting pun of the title *Idle Worship* attempts to raise the question of whether the growing pains involved in venerating rock gods and goddesses are worth the bother. Should we adore or abhor? Is what we see in our early pop role models a mirror, a mirage or a miracle? There is a war between romance and cynicism in this book, between faith and disillusionment. So it's just like *Tender Is the Night* really, okay?

It may have been André Breton who wrote 'Beauty will be convulsive or not at all,' but it was Patti Smith who put it on an album cover. It may have been Blondie who sang 'Dreaming is free,' but it was me who decided it would be a resonant end to this introduction. Go on, inspire yourself.

CHRIS ROBERTS, April 1994

You Gotta Have Lost a Couple o' Fights

Bono

im still starstruck, it doesn't wear off. . . frank sinatra gave
me a solid gold cartier pasha watch with sapphires and
an inscription. . . to bono with thanks FRANCIS A
SINATRA. . . WATER RESISTANT. . . im not gonna get
over this. . . Frank likes me. . . hell ive hung out with him,
drunk at his bar, eaten at his table, watched a movie at his
place. . . in his own screening room. . . dig that asshole. . .
i usually drink j.d. straight up without ice, its a tennessee
sipping whiskey, so why did i go and blow it by ordering
ginger ale. . . 'jack and ginger' a 'girls drink'. . . FRANK
looks at me and my two earrings and for the first time in my
life i felt effeminate. . . i drank quickly to compensate
and worse i mixed my drinks. . . over dinner (mexican not
italian) we drank tequila in huge fishbowl glasses, never
drink anything bigger than your head i thought as FRANK
pushed his nose up against the glass like it was a hall of
mirrors. . .

later asleep on the snowwhite of FRANK and BARBARA's
screening room sofa i had a real fright i woke up to wetness, ᴧᴧ

15

a damp sensation between my legs. . . hmm. . . dreams of dean martin gave way to panic. . . first thought: ive pissed myself. second: don't tell anyone. third: dont move theyll see the stain. . . yellow on white. fourth: make a plan. . . and so i sat in my shame for twenty minutes, mute, waiting for the movie to end, wondering as to how i would explain this. . . this. . . irish defeat to italy. . . this sign that what was once just verbal incontinence has matured. . . and grown to con-clusive proof that i didn't belong there/here. i am a jerk. i am a tourist, i am back in my cot age 4. . . before i knew how to fail – mama – ive pissed myself. . . again.

well i hadnt, id spilt my drink. i was drunk, high on him, a shrinking shadow boxing dwarf following in his footsteps. . . badly. . . STARSTRUCK. . . "what now my love? now that its over?" i went back to the hotel. . . (turn left on frank sinatra boulevard). i would never drink in the company of the great man again. . . i would never be asked to. wrong, twice.

NOTE: IF YOU'RE GONNA DROP ONE, DROP A BIG ONE. . . A NAME. . . A NAME TO HANG ON YOUR WALL. EPISODE NO. 1. december 93, u2 had just got back from TOKYO, the capitol of zoo tv, it was all over. . . i felt wonderful. i felt like shit. my TV had been turned off. . . it was christmas. . . there was a parcel from FRANK a large parcel. . . i opened it. . . a PAINTING, a painting by FRANK SINATRA and a note. . . 'you mentioned the jazz vibes in this piece well its called JAZZ and we'd like you to have it. yours Frank and Barbara' this is getting silly. . . there is a SANTA CLAUS and hes Italian. . . (opera, Fellini, food, wine, Positano, the sexy end of religion, football, now grace and generosity?). . . heroes are supposed to let you down. . . but here i am blown away by this 78 year-old saloon singer and his royal family. . . starstruck. . . a skunk on the outskirts of las vegas with my very own Frank Sinatra, last seen in his very own living room, on the edge of his very own desert, in palm springs. . . THE PAINTING, a luminous piece as complex as its title, as its author. . . circles closed yet interlocking, like glass stains on a beermat. . . circles with the diameter of a horn. . . Miles Davis. . . Buddy Rich. . . rhythm. . . the desert. . . theyre all in there. . . on yellow. . . to keep it mad. . . fly yourself to the moon!

EPISODE NO. 2 MARCH 1. im not an alcoholic im irish, i dont drink to get drunk do i? i drink because i like the taste dont i? so why am i drunk? im drunk because Frank has just fixed me another stiffy thats why! jack daniels this time straight up and in a pint glass.

its the 'Grammys' and ive been asked to present the boss of bosses with a life achievement award. . . a speech. . . i know im not match fit but of course i say yes.

and now im in NEW YORK CITY and so nervous i am deaf and cannot speak. . . two choices; BLUFF or concentrate on the job at hand, i do both and end up with a rambling wordy tribute with no fullstops or commas. . . that might explain how i felt about the man who invented pop music. . . and puncture the schmaltz. . . a little. . .

anyway we're in FS's dressing room (the manager's suite) where the small talk is never small, im talking to Susan Reynolds, Franks p.a. and patron saint and Ali (my wife and mine). Paul McGuinness (U2's manager) asks Frank about the pin on his lapel. . . 'its the legion of honor. . . highest civilian award. . . given by the president. . .' which one? enquires paul. . . 'oh i dont know. . . some old guy. . . i

think it was lincoln. . .' cool. . . do you have to be american
to get one? i think to myself. . . already feeling my legs
go. . .

next up the award for best alternative album u2 are nomi-
nated for this. . . better get ready. . . whats the point. . .
we're never gonna win that. . . that belongs to the smashing
pumpkins one of the few noisy bands to transcend the turgid
old-fashioned format theyve chosen. . . you have to go
downstairs. . . you might win . . .whats there to be embarrassed about. . . youve been no. 1 on alternative/college radio
for 10 years now. . . its the most important thing to you. . .
tell them. . . its your job to use your position. . . abuse
it even. . . tell them. . . you're not mainstream you're
slipstream. . . tell them. . . you'll make it more fun. . . that
you'll try to be better than the last lot. . . tell them you're
mainstream but not of it and that you'll do your best to fuck
it up. . . TELL THEM YOU KNOW FRANK. . . tell the
children. . . so i did.

the speechifying below wasn't heard in the uk so loud is the
word fuck over there but Frank heard it and Frank liked it. . .
so here it is:

Frank never did like rock 'n' roll. And he's not crazy about
guys wearing earrings either, but hey, he doesn't hold it
against me and anyway, the feeling's not mutual.

rock 'n' roll people love Frank Sinatra because Frank
Sinatra has got what we want. . . swagger and
ATTITUDE. . . HE'S BIG ON ATTITUDE. . . SERIOUS
ATTITUDE. . . BAD ATTITUDE. . . Franks THE
CHAIRMAN OF THE BAD.

rock 'n' roll plays at being tough, but this guy's. . . well,

he's the boss of bosses. The Man. The Big Bang of Pop.
I'M NOT GONNA MESS WITH HIM; ARE YOU?

who is this guy that every swingin city in america wants
to claim as their own?. this painter who lives in the desert,
this first-rate first-take actor, this singer who makes other
men poets, boxing clever with every word, talking like
america. . . Fast. . . straight up. . . in headlines. . . comin'
thru with the big schtick, the aside, the quiet compliment. . . good cop/bad cop in the same breath.

you know his story because it's your story. . . Frank walks
like America, COCKSURE. . .

Its 1945. . . the US cavalry are trying to get out of
Europe, but they never really do. They are part of another
kind of invasion. A.F.R. American Forces Radio, broad-
casting a music that will curl the stiff upper lip of England
and the rest of the world paving the way for Rock N' Roll
– with jazz, Duke Ellington, the big band, Tommy Dorsey,
and right out in front, FRANK SINATRA. . . his voice tight
as a fist, opening at the end of a bar not on the beat, over
it. . . playing with it, splitting it. . . like a jazz man, like
miles davis. . . turning on the right phrase in the right song,
which is where he lives, where he lets go, and where he
reveals himself. . . his songs are his home and he lets you
in. . . but you know. . . to sing like that, you gotta have
lost a couple o' fights. . . to know tenderness and romance
like that. . . you have to have had your heart broken.

people say Frank hasn't talked to the press. . . they want
to know how he is, whats on his mind. . . but y'know,
Sinatra is out there more nights than most punk bands. . .
selling his story through the songs, telling and articulate in
the choice of those songs. . . private thoughts on a public

address system. . . generous. . . this is the conundrum of frank sinatra left and right brain hardly talking, boxer and painter, actor and singer, lover and father. . . troubleshooter and troublemaker, bandman and loner, the champ who would rather show you his scars than his medals. . . he may be putty in barbaras hands but I'm not gonna mess with him are you?

LADIES AND GENTLEMEN, ARE YOU READY TO WELCOME A MAN HEAVIER THAN THE EMPIRE STATE, MORE CONNECTED THAN THE TWIN TOWERS, AS RECOGNISABLE AS THE STATUE OF LIBERTY. . . and LIVING PROOF THAT GOD IS A CATHOLIC. . . will you welcome THE KING OF NEW YORK CITY. . . FRANCIS. . . ALBERT . . . SINATRA.

Sparing the Rod

Nick Hornby

You want classic early seventies albums, I got 'em. The entire Al Green back catalogue, *Let's Get It On*, *There's No Place Like America Today*, *Grievous Angel*, *After the Goldrush*, *Blood on the Tracks* . . . Unimpeachable classics, every one, and while others may have to bury their Cat Stevens and James Taylor albums away when fashionable friends come round to borrow a cup of balsamic vinegar, I have nothing to hide. Those pre-Ramones years were difficult to pick your way through, but I seem to have managed it quite brilliantly. If there was a smarter, more forward-thinking, more retrospectively modish young teenager around than me between 1971 and 1975, I have yet to meet him.

Sadly, however, I am that commonplace phenomenon, Reinvented Man. Most of the Al Green back catalogue I bought in the early Eighties, the Gram Parsons at university in the late seventies, the Curtis Mayfield from a car boot sale a few years ago, and so on. I didn't buy any of them at the time of their release. I thought that soul music was for wide-boys, country was for old people, and Bob Dylan was for girls. ～

These are a few of the albums I bought back then: *McCartney*; *Led Zeppelin II*; a Humble Pie live double, the title of which escapes me; the Curved Air record which had painting on the vinyl; *Anyway* by Family; *Deep Purple in Rock*; *Tubular Bells*; a Van der Graaf Generator album, purchased after I read a review in *Melody Maker*, and if I ever meet the journalist who wrote the review he can either refund me my £2.19 or get biffed on the nose; *Rory Gallagher*; and *Every Picture Tells a Story*, by Rod Stewart.

Every Picture Tells a Story is the only one of those that I still possess. All of the others have disappeared, stolen or flogged (although the Van der Graaf Generator album was certainly not stolen, and I can't imagine who would have bought it off me); some of them were flogged because I needed the money, others because they had absolutely no place in the ineffably cool collection I was in the process of assembling.

So how come Rod Stewart has survived? 'Now there was someone who never let you down,' a friend remarked sardonically when I owned up to my tragic affliction, and he has a point. Rod's track record is not without its blemishes. There was Britt Ekland, for a start. And tartan. And 'Ole Ola', his 1978 Scotland World Cup Song (the chorus – and I may be misquoting, but not by much – went something like 'Ole Ole, Ole Ola/We're going to bring the World Cup back from over thar'). And 'D'Ya Think I'm Sexy'. And the Faces live album *Overture and Beginners*, which the NME commemorated with its annual 'Rod Stewart and the Faces Thanks-For-the-Live-Album-Lads-But-You-Really-Shouldn't-Have-Bothered Award'. (The record ends with Stewart thanking the audience 'for your time . . . and your money', and you really have to hear the lascivious drawl in his voice to appreciate the full horror of the moment.) And the haircut. And his obsession with LA. And the champagne and straw boaters on album sleeves. And 'Sailing', which made a pretty decent football song but an interminable single. And several other blonde women who weren't Britt Ekland but might as well have been. And the couplet from the song 'Italian Girls' (on *Never a Dull Moment*) that goes: 'I was feeling kind of silly/When I stepped in some Caerphilly'. And the cover of the record *Ooh La La*, a pathetically cheap arrangement which allowed the purchaser to jiggle a tab and make a man's eyes go up and down in a supposedly hilarious manner. And the record itself, arguably the worst collection of songs ever released by anybody. And the all-purpose session-musician sub-Stones rock'n'roll plod-raunch that can be found on any of his post-Faces work, 'Hot Legs' being the template. And the Faces live shows, which were apt to end with the entire band lying in a drunken heap on the stage. He's hardly put a foot wrong, really.

I bought *Every Picture Tells a Story* in the Virgin shop in Oxford Street: there was only one Virgin shop then, situated right where the Megastore is now, except you had to walk through a shoe shop (or rather, a cowboy boot shop) and up some stairs to get to it. I lived thirty miles from Oxford Street, but this was still my nearest discount record store, and though the train fare cancelled out any savings I made, it was much more fun buying records there. There were headphones, and beanbags (although the beanbags were frequently occupied by dossers) and bootlegs, which I had never seen before.

And in any case, the length of the journey lent a proper gravity to the serious business of record-buying. Now, I indulge myself whenever I feel like it, even in times when I have had no money at all; there are occasions over the last fifteen or so years when I have come back home yet again with a square-shaped carrier bag and felt sick with guilt and over-consumption. ('I haven't even played side two of the album I bought after work on Tuesday, so how come I've bought another one today?') In those Virgin days, I thought and read and talked for weeks before committing myself to something I would have to live with and listen to for months. (Mistakes, like the Van der Graaf Generator record, had to be paid for by the self-flagellation of listening to the wretched thing and kidding myself that I liked it.)

Every Picture Tells a Story seemed a safe bet. I had heard 'Maggie May', of course, and knew that any album featuring a song like that would not be actively unpleasant; I could count on songs, and singing, and these seemed like reassuring virtues. And songs and singing was what I got: 'Maggie May', 'Reason to Believe', a beautiful cover of a Dylan song, 'Tomorrow is a Long Time', a decent stab at the Temptations' 'I Know I'm Losing You' (I didn't really approve of Rod singing a song by a Tamla Motown group – Motown was for sisters and people like that – but there were plenty of guitars, so I let it pass) . . . loads of stuff. There wasn't anything I didn't like, really. I played *Every Picture Tells a Story* to death, and then let it rest in peace.

But, like all the best teen icons, Rod wasn't a mere recording artiste, he was a lifestyle. You couldn't just listen to his music, forget about him, and put him away in the little and chronically over-familiar pile of records in your bedroom (I probably had about nine albums by then, and in truth I was pretty sick of all of them). He *resonated*. For a start, there was this football thing he had. At school, the sight of him kicking balls into the 'Top of the Pops' audience excited a great deal of favourable comment; ever since punk, it has been *de rigueur* for bands to express an interest in the people's game, but back then, things were different, mostly because of the kind of music I was listening to. Few of the people I watched football with at Arsenal looked as if they knew who Humble Pie were; none of the people I watched Humble Pie with cared how Arsenal had got on. (I remember John Peel attempting to read out the football results at a late-summer Hyde Park concert, *and getting booed for doing so*.) When I went to see the Who, I saw that rock and football did not have to attract entirely separate audiences, but for the most part, the Afghans at the gigs and the Crombies at the grounds never got to rub against each other; Rod Stewart was a godsend to the countless teenage boys who couldn't see why Ron Wood and Ron Harris should have to live on different planets.

And it was much easier to *be* Rod Stewart than it was to be Hendrix or Jagger or Jim Morrison. Tartan scarves were easier to find in Maidenhead than leather trousers, and Rod had never worn a dress, like Jagger had. There was no need to take heroin, or read Rimbaud, or play a guitar with your teeth, or know who Meher Baba was; all you needed to do to acquire Rodness was drink, sing, pick up girls and like football. It was easy. We could all do that without having to go to LA or even Soho. (We weren't drinking or picking up girls yet, needless to say, or at least not properly, if you catch my drift. But we would, no problem, no need to worry about us, pal.) The photo on the gatefold sleeve of *Never a Dull Moment* depicted Stewart's band lined up in a goalmouth; on *Smiler*, they were all raising pints outside a suitably cor-blimey looking pub. This was transparently shameless stuff and it is impossible to look at these photos now without cringing; we were being conned rotten, but we didn't know that then, and even if we did we wouldn't have cared.

I went to see the Faces in 1971, at the Oval, but I cannot remember so much as a bum Ronnie Wood note now. (And the next time I saw them, at the Reading Festival, they left no impression either. This may well have been a result of their liberal pre-gig refreshment policy.) In 1972, when I was fifteen, there was 'You Wear It Well', which, reassuringly, sounded exactly the same as 'Maggie May', but with its own tune, and the album *Never a Dull Moment*, and the Faces album *A Nod's as Good as a Wink*, and the single 'Stay With Me', and the single 'What's Made Milwaukee Famous', which came in a tartan picture sleeve, and the Python Lee Jackson single 'In A Broken Dream', which became the traditional bottom-groping finale to every village hall disco I went to. I didn't need to think about any other pop singers; there was enough Rod Stewart product to soak up all the record-buying money I had. (It was no use being a Stones fan, or a Dylan fan, or a Floyd fan – you had to wait *years*.) *A Nod's as Good as a Wink* was dreadful, the usual admixture of tired Chuck Berryisms, duff lyrics and a chronic fluff-on-the-needle production; I didn't even like 'Stay With Me' that much, although it was OK if you wanted to pretend to share a microphone with a pal (then – as now, as far as I am able to tell from 'The Chart Show' – you leaned back, head on one side, with the arm furthest from the mike punching the air).

The solo stuff was different, much more tender, and certainly more wrought. The booze-and-football photos, it is clear now, were intended to compensate for the rampant sissiness of the recordings, the Bob Dylan covers ('Mama You Been on

My Mind', 'Girl from the North Country'), the McCartney ballads ('Mine for Me'), and Stewart's own sentimental cod-Celtic songs. This was the stuff I preferred; indeed, I would still rather listen to a ballad than anything else, and maybe this is Rod's legacy to me.

They still sound surprisingly good, those three solo albums (*Every Picture . . .*, *Never a Dull Moment* and *Smiler*) that created the Hampden-and-bitter Stewart image. The cover versions are immaculate: so good, in fact, that when I sought out the originals (during that purist phase all Music Blokes go through, when we believe that originals must by definition be superior to the copies), I was disappointed by them. Sam Cooke's 'Bring It on Home to Me' didn't have that rollicking string arrangement; Dylan's 'Mama You Been on My Mind' was pretty but plain, and anyway Dylan couldn't sing.

And Stewart's voice still sounds great. Why Caucasians used to believe that rock stars with croaky voices – Stewart, Janis Joplin, Frankie Miller, Joe Cocker, Paul Young – are white soul singers remains one of life's impenetrable mysteries. (During the eighties, thankfully, with the advent of the more honey-toned George Michael and Boy George, this perplexing claim ceased to be made.) Only the overrated Otis Redding sounds as though he is gargling through porridge; neither Al Green nor Marvin Gaye nor Aretha Franklin seems as distressed, as pained, as the Croakies. Surely one of the points of soul singing is its effortlessness? But Stewart pinches other things from black music traditions: his vocal mannerisms, his laughs and spoken asides, and the way he rides the beat and slides under and over the melody line . . . these are the tell-tale signs of somebody with a good record collection and a sharp pair of ears, and they set him apart from the opposition.

And anyway, Stewart had grown up with folk (hence the Dylan and the Tim Hardin covers) as well as the more ubiquitous R&B. He wasn't a Jagger or an Elton John, but a straightforward, uncomplicated interpreter of popular songs: fifteen years earlier, he might have been our answer to Dean Martin; fifteen years later, he probably would have been a one-hit wonder for Stock, Aitken and Waterman.

Things went downhill fast after *Smiler*. There was one great last Faces single, 'You Can Make Me Dance, Sing or Anything', which swung in a way that most English rock songs do not (mostly, I discovered years later, because Stewart and Wood had liberated a huge chunk of a Bobby Womack song for their fade-out), and then the band split up. Ronnie Wood joined the Rolling Stones, a move which, distressingly, made a lot of sense. And a year or so later *Atlantic Crossing* was released. There was no football pitch or pub photo on the sleeve of this one: just a monstrous cartoon drawing of Stewart, wearing an improbable silver jump-suit and, well, crossing the Atlantic.

I had left school by this time. And I had also turned my back on the other Rod fans I had knocked around with in the fourth and fifth forms: I was off to university and they weren't, and I had started to hang around with people who made jokes about Existentialism (admittedly, the jokes consisted mainly of saying the word aloud, but they would not have amused the people with whom I had once shared an imaginary microphone). Had Rod met Britt by then? I don't remember. And in any case, Britt was not to blame for the self-parody which sucked Rod down and out; if it hadn't been her, it would have been someone else – Farrah Fawcett, maybe, or some Seventies equivalent of that woman who knocks around with

Michael Winner. Rod was hell-bent on making a berk of himself, and he didn't need any help from Scandinavian bit-part actresses.

I bought *Atlantic Crossing* anyway, for its two aching ballads, 'I Don't Want to Talk About It' and 'It's Not the Spotlight', but it was the weakest of his solo work – and therefore of the entire Stewart oeuvre – to date. And then I went to college, and listened to punk and blues and soul and reggae, and it should have stopped there, but it didn't. My devotion intensified: I wore a Rod Stewart T-shirt that I'd bought for 50p, and I had a Rod Stewart poster on the wall of my college bedroom. It was, I guess, an ironic devotion – Rod had become a post-punk figure of fun by that time, and you would have to have been particularly imbecilic not to get the joke – but there was a glimmer of earnestness there, too: I was frightened by the Athena prints of Renoir and Matisse paintings that hung on my neighbours' walls, and of the classical music that I occasionally heard coming from their stereos, and used Rod as a kind of talisman to protect me from these evil and alien forces. So I stuck with it for a while, until I felt more comfortable with University and with myself, and then I gave up. I preferred the Tom Waits version of 'Downtown Train' – he still listens, you have to give him credit for that – and I haven't even bothered with the *Unplugged* album, which seemed aimed straight at me, and those like me.

But these are the records I own because of Rod: *His California Album*, by Bobby Bland, which is where Stewart first heard 'It's Not the Spotlight' (and though Stewart's version is flatter and less piquant than Bland's, Rod wisely didn't bother with Bland's unattractive trademark phlegm-clearing whoops), and maybe even 'If Loving You Is Wrong (I Don't

Want to Be Right)'; my entire Bobby Womack collection; my
Chuck Berry's Golden Decade; my *Temptations' Greatest
Hits*; and my Sam Cooke album. I was introduced to the Isley
Brothers ('This Old Heart of Mine'), Aretha Franklin ('You
Make Me Feel Like a Natural Woman/Man'), and Crazy Horse
('I Don't Want to Talk about It'). And once I had been introduced to Aretha Franklin and Bobby Bland and the Temptations and Chuck Berry, I got to know B.B. King and the Four
Tops and Atlantic Records and Chess Records and . . . He
gave me a good start in life, and as a young man, a pop innocent, one cannot ask for anything more than that. If I had
been similarly smitten by Elton John or James Taylor or Jethro
Tull or Mike Oldfield, all of whom were competing for attention at around the same time, it is possible that I would have
junked my entire record collection a decade or so ago.

The people who stick with pop the longest, it seems to me
now, are those who entrust themselves at a tender age to
somebody like Stewart, somebody who loves and listens to
pop music. Those who fell for the Stones got to hear, if they
could be bothered, Arthur Alexander and Solomon Burke and
Don Covay (and if they got to hear Don Covay they would find
themselves wondering what, precisely, Jagger had brought to
the Sixties party). Those who went for Led Zeppelin went on
to Muddy Waters and Howlin' Wolf. Genesis and Pink Floyd
led you up a blind alley: there was nowhere to go, and so a
good many people I knew stopped dead. Today's youngsters,
eh? Where are they heading for after they've chewed up the
Sisters of Mercy or the Happy Mondays? (Suede and Teenage
Fanclub, on the other hand . . .) Even after all these years,
even after Britt and 'D'Ya Think I'm Sexy' and blah blah blah,
I'd still like to buy Rod a drink; I'd like to sit him down and

talk to him, not about Celtic or Jock Stein or Denis Law or ligaments or real ale, but about music. He knows much more than he's ever let on.

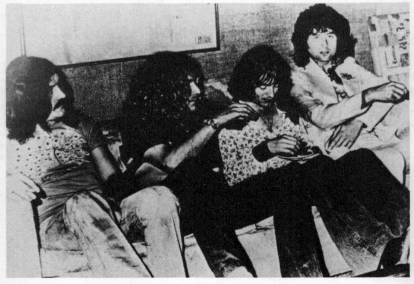

Led Zeppelin and the Pixies

Martin Millar

IN 1972, WHEN I WAS A YOUNG TEENAGER living in Glasgow, I did not expect Led Zeppelin to come to town. I had been going to gigs since I was thirteen and as Glasgow was a popular venue for music I had already seen most of the biggest progressive rock bands of the day – Hawkwind, Black Sabbath, Captain Beefheart, Mott the Hoople, Alex Harvey, Deep Purple, The Who, and many more. (With great foolishness I declined to go and see T. Rex, deeming them to be too poppy. How silly can you get?) Nonetheless, I did not expect Led Zeppelin to come. They were too big, and too serious. I mean, they didn't release singles or anything.

I had no clear idea of what the daily life of Led Zeppelin might be and assumed vaguely that they lived in some sort of Valhalla, sipping mead, talking to the muses and occasionally making records. Possibly they granted a few divine favours in between times. Whatever they did it would not include touring Scotland because, at least in my school, Led Zeppelin were a class apart, and we were not worthy.

People, including me, used to marvel that anything as good

as them could possibly exist. We used to walk around the playground carrying their albums despite the fact that there was nowhere in school to play them. It was just good to have them around, and be seen with them. I spent a fair part of my early youth walking back and forth clutching *Led Zeppelin Two*, singing the riff to 'Whole Lotta Love' and conscientiously imitating all the guitar solos. (I bought this record before I had a record player. Really.)

This for me is the stuff of strong memories. For instance, when *Led Zeppelin Four* was released the first reports were confused. Two separate people who had skipped school for the day reported that they had seen it in shop windows but each of their descriptions of the album sleeve was radically different. This led us to wild and lengthy speculations in class ranging from the likelihood of two Led Zeppelin albums being simultaneously released to one of the sightseers being strongly affected by LSD, which was always a possibility in the early seventies, even among the very young.

Strangely enough, the solution turned out to be that one shop was displaying one side of the sleeve and the other shop was showing the other. It was of course a mighty and complex gatefold sleeve, the like of which is no longer to be seen in these post-heroic days. Such was our immense Led Zeppelin interest that this sort of thing was fuel for hours and hours of fevered discussion which I still recall though I have no idea what I might have been supposed to be learning in the class at the time.

I think it was shortly after this that we heard that they were coming to play in Glasgow. Now for me, already hurt and disillusioned in life because other boys had girlfriends and I had no idea how to go about this, my main happiness and only spiritual elevation was obtained by lying around in incense-filled rooms, listening to Led Zeppelin. The prospect of seeing them live was therefore overwhelming.

I queued up overnight for my ticket. The police patrolling this queue were particularly and needlessly unpleasant but I will not dwell on this as I do not wish to spoil the memory. The venue was Green's Playhouse, later to become the Apollo. This had several features which would annoy me now, namely it did not sell alcohol and it was seated but I don't recall being troubled by this at the time. Everyone generally stood on the seats or rushed to the front when the band played. As to alcohol, this was more of a problem, particularly as we were all too young to buy it legally elsewhere. Much creative thinking was done to obtain a few cans of McEwans and it was necessary to drink them quickly and surreptitiously in the street before the gig. Many junior rock fans, forced to bolt down their beer in the short distance between the bus stop and the venue, paid a heavy price later in terms of illness, disorientation and utterly irate parents.

I have probably never been as excited as when waiting for Led Zeppelin to come onstage. In the weeks since buying the tickets I had talked of little else. Well, probably nothing else. Although everybody had their different preferred bands we were entirely united in regarding Led Zeppelin as by far the best, apart from the out and out pop music fans, of whom I seem to remember there were relatively few, and possibly one or two hard-core West Coast devotees. To this day I completely fail to understand what they saw in Crosby, Stills, Nash and Young. I mean, put 'Our House' next to 'Black Dog' and what have you got? Precious little if you ask me.

It was not unknown for bands to cancel their trips to

Glasgow and this had been a source of great dread. Grimly pessimistic even at an early age, I was more or less convinced that they would not appear. Right up till the moment that Robert Plant, my complete, total and absolute adolescent hero, stepped onstage, I did not actually believe that they would play.

Now the Glasgow audience, while appreciative, usually took some time to warm up. Generally they would spend some suspicious moments sizing up the band before completely accepting them. Even then any heavy rock outfit indulging in too much balladeering and not enough power chords could be given a fairly hard time. On this night this was not the case. As Led Zeppelin appeared onstage like Mighty Heroes From Another Realm the place exploded. Everyone was up over the seats and piling down the front before Jimmy Page had completed his first riff. The bouncers, hardened Glasgow thugs normally hostile to this sort of behaviour, retreated in confusion.

Led Zeppelin played with no support act and, unlike many of the other bands in the fab early seventies, had no stage set and no fancy clothes. They wore plain T-shirts and jeans and their onstage equipment looked fairly modest although Robert Plant did have a sort of metal stick which made funny noises when he put his hands near it, very important for the psychedelic middle section of 'Whole Lotta Love'.

They started off with 'Black Dog', a song with a dazzlingly good riff, and from then on it just got better. Thundering versions of crunching tunes like 'The Immigrant Song', 'Communication Breakdown' and 'Rock and Roll' flowed into the powerful electric blues of 'Killing Floor' and 'I Can't Quit You Babe'. (I suppose I would now have to grudgingly admit that it was a bad thing for Led Zeppelin not to have immediately acknowledged the original versions of some of these blues. At the time I would not have cared. I mean the original artists played them quietly, with acoustic guitars. Not the same thing at all.)

There were the screaming vocals of Robert Plant and the wailing and fantastical guitar playing of Jimmy Page. Behind them, as we young rock completists were well aware after dutifully sending in our poll forms for 'Musician of the Year' in each category to the music papers, were the excellent John Bonham on drums and the equally excellent John Paul Jones playing bass and keyboards. In between the huge chunks of noise were outbreaks of calm as they played a few acoustic numbers and some gentle songs of Misty Mountains and Elvish Warriors, all this being well suited to alleviating the tedium and frustration of my youthful existence. Aware of the status of the band, the audience listened to these in quiet rapture and did not speak, cough or fidget.

I loved every second of it. I was enormously appreciative of John Bonham's drum solo. When Jimmy Page played his guitar with a violin bow I quite possibly wept for joy. I think it is an accurate recollection, rather than wishful thinking, that Led Zeppelin did do extremely good live versions of their material. As 'Whole Lotta Love' climaxed I had reached the sort of state you see in films of early Beatles concerts, that is, more or less hysterical. Seeing Led Zeppelin was probably a more satisfying fulfilment of a dream than any that was to follow.

They ended with 'Stairway to Heaven'. Wow. What experience could have been better for me and my schoolfriends? None. Nothing would have come close. It was the best song in the world played by the best band in the world and here they were doing it right in front of us. The Archangel Gabriel coming onstage and blowing his trumpet would have had less effect. The concert ended. I was awestruck.

Outside I was completely deafened but still awestruck. That night the deafness gave way to a hideous ringing in my ears and I was still awestruck. Next day at school everyone was awestruck.

'We are awestruck,' we said, walking around the playground carrying our Led Zeppelin albums. 'Completely awestruck.'

And it was true.

Time moves on. A few years later I was no longer awestruck by Led Zeppelin. They released another good album, *Physical Graffiti*, but were overtaken by time and the Sex Pistols. I went to many punk concerts, and it was still enjoyable but as the eighties crept on I started to lose the habit.

I was, I suppose, a little bored with the whole thing. Music did not seem a great deal of fun. I was aware however that this was a problem with me rather than the music. It is odd how people can dismiss whatever is popular at the time as 'not as good as it was in my day' and actually make themselves believe it. There is always something good around, it's just that you get past the stage of appreciating it properly. Personally I was a little distressed no longer to appreciate it properly. Having passed thirty it always seemed like too much effort to actually go and see a band anywhere, what with London being so difficult to travel around in late at night. It was also too much effort to enter enthusiastically the fantasy land of any group of people whose sole talent was knocking together a reasonable tune and posing onstage. I had probably not been really excited by a live band since The Jesus and Mary Chain some years previously and by 1989 I had ceased going to gigs entirely.

By 1989 of course music listening had entirely changed. Whereas at my school Led Zeppelin were common currency, by now no such common currency existed. In any school there would be devotees of Heavy Metal, Rap, Reggae, Trance, Techno, Thrash, Hardcore, Indie Rock and no doubt various others. Dance music, utterly without credibility in the early seventies, was now popular with all sorts of people. However as this is a piece about two gigs rather than a history of music I shall pass over this, merely pointing out that from my point of view, proper music absolutely requires that there should be someone onstage hitting a loud guitar and the guitar has to be plugged into a fuzzbox. Anything else just won't do.

So, where was I? Living in London and gone completely off gigs, it would seem. And I must admit that this was somewhat of a disappointment, and made me feel old.

When someone provided me with a spare ticket for the Pixies in 1989 I accepted it fairly doubtfully. I really only agreed to go at all because my pleasant new girlfriend wanted to. Personally I would just as soon have stayed home watching TV, especially as Britain's late-night viewing had radically improved in recent years and I could now watch all night 'American Gladiators' and 'Video Fashion'.

I had no great expectations of the music. For one thing, I had never heard the Pixies. They were American and had been in Britain before but this was their first time as stars. Their first full album, *Surfer Rosa*, was a big hit and they were receiving a lot of attention. So although I was ignorant of them, among others there was an air of expectation about the gig generated by those hip enough to have bought their first release, *Come On Pilgrim*, a mini LP, and those still avidly tuning in to John Peel on the radio.

Life for me now was different of course. I had to work for a living, which was bad. On the other hand, I no longer had to make up stories and bribe older people to buy me alcohol, which was good. I was fully entitled to march into any bar in London and demand a pint, and a whisky to follow if I deemed it necessary. I had my own home to go to and would not be censored by anyone even if I crawled through the door and made a mess on the carpet.

Different as well was my attitude to the upcoming event. I did not hang around in my bedroom listening obsessively to Pixies records, as I did in those weeks preceding Led Zeppelin's show. Nor did I talk about the gig continually, or feverishly worry that it might be cancelled. I probably would not have minded had it been cancelled. This would have saved me the trouble of going out and left me free to watch 'American Gladiators' and 'Video Fashion'. How perilous it can be to reach thirty!

The concert was at the Town and Country Club – a very strange name for a music venue I always thought. Unable to come up with any last-minute excuse for staying in, I reluctantly got myself ready and found myself packed in with what seemed like hundreds of people in a Transit van, driving slowly from Brixton to Kentish Town.

As I crawled out of the van, and rubbed the circulation back into my limbs, I saw that there were people everywhere. Hordes of fans were struggling out of the Bull and Gate, pint glasses still in hand, and queueing up for the Town and Country. The pavements were full of couples holding hands, groups of young boys and girls edging their way closer to the doors, serious looking souls selling fanzines, gloomy-faced policemen, hopeful ticket touts, and various smug-looking people slipping in through the door marked Guest Passes. All in all a good atmosphere, and I was already thinking that possibly this was not such a bad thing to be doing.

The Town and Country was a good venue, much better than Green's Playhouse, with bars in easy access, a huge open space to hang around in and a balcony with seats if you needed a rest. As we arrived the support act was playing. I have never had any interest at all in support acts, regarding them mainly as things that get in the way of the real gig, but tonight it was My Bloody Valentine and they were very fine. Already a fair proportion of the crowd was dancing to their dense sound.

All around young Pixies devotees filled up with lager, bought T-shirts and waited impatiently for the moment. Had they been waiting anxiously for weeks to see the band? Had they discussed in intimate detail with their friends the precise meanings of the songs? Did they love the Pixies the way I had loved Led Zeppelin? Quite possibly.

Now to love a band it is of course necessary to wish to enter their world. Whilst at school I had no trouble in imagining myself entering the Tolkienesque bar-room of Led Zeppelin but seventeen years later it was not the sort of thing I did any more. Despite all this good atmosphere I may well have sat upstairs quietly for the whole night had it not been for the unexpected charisma of Black Francis, the Pixies singer, and the strange and attractive world he created. There was definitely something pleasantly weird about the Pixies and it was apparent the moment they came onstage. Perhaps it was the peculiar sexuality in their lyrics, or the small but noticeable aberrations in their four/four timing, or their determinedly unglamorous but imposing stage presence, or maybe just the fact that some of their lyrics were in Spanish. I think I favour the last alternative. Already heavily under the influence of the excellent *Love and Rockets* comic where really cool young Hispanics hung around being bored, having fun and playing in bands, I could easily imagine myself embroiled in serious love affairs with señoritas under the parching sun of a Mexican desert. Huge cacti dominate the landscape, and maybe men with shotguns.

As 'Levitation' roared out from the stage I found myself nodding my head. When they started up on 'Gigantic' I was tapping my feet and by the time they played 'Broken Face' I was elbowing young whippersnappers out of the way on my way down to the front. And once there, what enjoyment. The Pixies really did create the strangest world, a mixture of screeching guitars, enticingly bad sex and Latin banditry. This they wrapped around their own slightly off-centre thundering beat and it sounded a lot more effective than any other band I had heard for a long time.

Black Francis, huge charisma in hand, roared out his strange fantasies of receiving female clothing through the mail or losing his penis to a whore with diseases. Beside him Joey Santiago played loudly through a fuzzbox, exactly as required. Kim Deal played an excellent bass and sang some as well and I still retain enough of the teenage trainspotter mentality to report that the drummer was also good, and his name was David Lovering. The whole audience danced, drank and had a good time, and so did I.

I later discovered that *Surfer Rosa* is a very fine record, but live the songs sounded even better. I had no trouble at all in believing in the world they created. If Black Francis was off to plead his case with whores behind huge desert cacti, I was quite prepared to go with him.

It was extremely hot. I was dripping with sweat. To my great delight I remembered that this sort of thing was fun.

As much fun as Led Zeppelin? Well, maybe not. After all, you can't keep having teenage dreams fulfilled all your life. But more fun than going to the pictures, or watching TV, or sitting in a bar, or playing video games, or eating in restaurants, or writing.

My pleasant new girlfriend and I were happy as we returned home. Next day I went out and bought *Surfer Rosa*, and later I bought a bootleg tape of the gig. I also started reading music papers again, and listening to the John Peel show, not wishing to miss any new Pixies records.

And that is it, really. Since then I have not neglected to go to gigs, and I continue to have fun. Now if you are the sort of person who never felt old at all when you found you were thirtysomething, then I expect that this will have no meaning. But if you're that sort of person, to hell with you anyway. As far as I am concerned my gig-going days were rescued by the Pixies, and I will still be struggling my way through the doors way into my twilight years.

:‖ Vedder as Merton: 2001

Stephen J. Malkmus

Dear Father Flye,

I am on my way to visit Eddie Vedder at his secluded monastery in the Tennessee Hills. I am working on a paper about the Holy Spirit Explosion of the 1830s. During this era the Methodist Church split in half and the Baptists went four different ways. New and radical faiths sprouted up all over the country. Vedder is an expert in Shaker and Mormon history and I have a feeling he will be able to fill me in on what caused all the fuss.

Eddie and I have corresponded for many years since the fabled break-up of his group, Pearl Jam. We began our friendship when I was in exile on the island of Crete; Eddie had a keen interest in a Christian mystic who lived near my flat. He was believed to have healing powers – all sorts of folk came to him for help: Turkish lepers, Society mavens with breast cancer . . . even Rod Stewart! I spent a lot of time spying on the compound, and Eddie was quite grateful to me for the vivid descriptions I sent to him. Perhaps that is why he agreed to see me; from what I understand he is sort of a hermit these days.

〜

He never gave a concrete answer as to why he quit Pearl Jam. Our friendship has little to do with music (at least modern 'pop' music – I do remember writing to him about the jaded easy-listening craze of the early 1990s and the cult of domesticity in the upper echelons of the music industry). At any rate it seems as time goes on that the bitterness about the Pearl Jam Thing has washed over him, and I expect him to be in good spirits when I reach the monastery.

Eddie is fascinated by the rise of the Mormon Church. Mormonism is filled with weird rationalizations; its iconography, to the lay observer, can only be considered perverse. One thing you can say about the Mormons: they laid the groundwork. The collective sweat of the Mormon Church could fill Salt Lake. The twentieth century has seen their ranks swell – it is a wonder there are enough individual Spirit-Worlds to go around.

I once dreamed of starting a religion. Ho-hum. But along with professional polo and vodka tasting I gave it up for a more practical life. In fact it was Eddie who convinced me that the last thing this world needed was another religion. He had experienced a most peculiar ascension; through sheer denial of his place in the world he was sainted by major publications across the globe (*Rolling Stone*, *Spex*). The emotion, the honesty, the astrological concurrence – Eddie seemed peculiarly intense. I myself remember hearing his voice and thinking it belonged in a church instead of on stage. And I don't mean just the choir, for there were many groups back then that copped religio-spiritual imagery (Afghan Whigs, Spacemen 3, Natalie Cole). But Eddie and Eddie only seemed like he belonged in the pulpit, the word just passing through him like from some other place.

God cared so much about music he put it in the Bible. He knew about sympathetic vibrations; the hymns uplift our western souls. Pearl Jam songs are even less catchy than hymns yet managed to be quite popular in 1993 – the world must have been very suspicious of a good melody back then. Only when melody is the devil can Stone Temple Pilots be the saviour. It gets in the way of the message, and that was the one thing that a band needed (needs) to ascend, a message. And since Pearl Jam's message seemed to be the most authentic, since Eddie's words seemed to be channelled from somewhere else, we were especially sympathetic to the music.

The year is 2001, and it feels more and more like 1993. If there was ever a better time to start a religion I would like to know when. We have seen eight years of complacency. No one has been willing to step up and really make a stand. U2 traded the Gaza strip for Ireland as their favourite charity organization and disappeared. The lawsuit between Mark Eitzel and Pearl Jam sapped the soul out of the alternative music scene; it became evident that nothing was sacred when money came into the picture.

By 1995 all we were left with were the *faux*-historical bands – Suede, Teenage Fanclub, Stereolab, The Palace Brothers. They told us a lot about linear thought but the message was sad and reductive: music can't teach us anything we don't already know. At least their songs were good, which is more than you can say for most groups.

It reminds me of so many other cycles of history. Take the art world in the 1970s. The seventies were consumed by performance art. With 'painting is dead' came obvious stagnation in the art world. Painting could go no farther, history was over, avant-garde was bullshit (every rebellion is co-opted and in fifty years is seen as a natural progression from what came before). So much for revvvolution.

But in the early eighties along came the 'superstar artists' – Clemente, Salle, Schnabel et al. They boldly declared to the art-buying public: 'Painting is not Dead.' They painted these giant canvasses that signified SUBLIME but filled them with meaningless images and a couple of crucial art-historical references. History continues! So these paintings cried; in fact, that was the only real message they contained. As we know the artists became fabulously rich. Galleries pre-sold their paintings for upwards of a quarter of a million dollars. Cash through history.

Of course by 1993 we could see through their shabby act. No painter would be caught dead painting in that ostentatious 1980 style. Artists instead opted for Pearl Jam-style piety, albeit with more obvious canon-fucking and PC justification for their creations.

But the fact that Salle, Schnabel et al. put this over on so many people should be inspiration for any charlatan who wants to start a religion (or a rock band). For once the art world established the reputations of these artists, as soon as they were the 'saviours', their works could not be criticized. If you cut down Salle and you owned one of his *faux*-misogynistic canvasses, you stood to lose both face and money. If you criticized Mormonism's founder Joseph Smith because he wanted to sleep with your wife, you could burn in hell.

So much for the evangelical impulse in the arts. Suede is Salle. Urge Overkill is Koons. Eddie is just Eddie: no wonder he quit.

The Pearl Jam spirit-world seemed so fresh and exciting in 1993. It beckoned the family of man, not just the family of rock-likers . . . Eddie as the ideal Adam-lad, weaned on some sort of anti-Axl Southern California trip. Perfect media match for a guilty planet.

I will never forget when Vedder threw in the towel. Two weeks of touring with Urge Overkill is a lot to ask of anybody and I can imagine Eddie was not of sound mind and body by the time he got to Phoenix. He announced to a capacity crowd in the Phoenix Sundome that Pearl Jam was total failure. 'You won't see me up here again,' he declared, and walked off the stage.

Arizona could bum just about anyone out, don't you think? The place is overrun by snowbirds and the Sun City Girls have been on House Arrest at the Hanford Nuclear Reservations since 1999. The twenty-first century motto of Arizona is 'Factoid Centra for the Lost Midwest'.

Eddie had had enough of the charade. I sympathise with him. I feel his pain too. I remember a letter he wrote me. King Roeser, the guitarist for Urge Overkill (who is solely responsible for breaking up more groups than anyone other than Steve Vai), said something to Eddie which really bummed him out. It concerned the hymn 'O Come All Ye Faithful'.

'O COME ALL YE FAITHFUL JOYFUL AND TRIUMPHANT'
FAITHFUL: The fans.
JOYFUL: Epic Records, Pearl Jam's management company.
TRIUMPHANT: Pearl Jam themselves.

I can tell you from the letters I received that Eddie was hardly triumphant. He constantly assumed the voice of a guilty saint. When you are humble enough to realize that you are no better than any other person and that your elevated place in the world is due to luck, timing and a record company that profits tenfold compared to what you earn, you feel guilty (regardless of individual talent or hard work, these things are necessary for the cultural power that the five Pearl Jam boys have earned so quickly).

Quitting is noble. Big Black and Scratch Acid saw it that way at least. When a band decides to pack in the other bands whisper secret sighs of relief – 'ahhhhh, one less band to compete against.' That Stone Temple Pilots singer did not have to act out his Vedder-Oedipus fantasy after all; like a good father Eddie did it for him in a basketball arena in Phoenix.

I know it is difficult to see Rock and Roll as a moral battleground. We heard so much about the Led Zep coke parties, the Wild Perverted rockers of the fifties and sixties, and the bluesmen who sold their souls to the devil. The nineties saw a new rock piety rise up against Rod Stewart and his ten gallons of come. Only marijuana survived the revolution. So many musicians needed the stuff for inspiration that they could just not make an issue of it. As you know marijuana has survived to this very day and it makes me wonder if it might not be such a bad thing after all.

Father Flye, I hope you are not offended by my forthright opinions. It is a different kind of thing to what I am used to doing when I write to you. I just saw an old interview with that fellow who hosted 'The Gong Show'. He said something to the effect of television being critic-proof because no-one has to pay to watch it. Only when people have to pull money out of their pockets do they care if they are spending it on something objectively worthwhile (although we know critics are never objective and that you pay for television in the long run one way or another, you get my drift.) Perhaps that is the kind of writing I would like to do. It would be nice to be paid to do something that had absolutely no influence on the world whatsoever. I guess it is impossible if you are a nit-picker because every action causes a reaction. Guitar players are for the most part worthless creatures but at least they make the strings vibrate.

I suppose you would not remember this but I feel like telling you about it. Do you remember that rock group the Psychedelic Furs? They had a few minor hits back in the eighties. I saw the lead singer in a café. He was interviewing eager young guitarists. Maybe he is getting a band together. I remember that Psychedelic Furs box set that came out around New Year was considered a commercial failure, although how they decide it's a failure after only ten months is a mystery to me.

I leave you with a war poem by James Agee.

We Soldiers of All Nations Who Lie Killed

We soldiers of all nations who lie killed
Ask little: that you never, in our name,
Dare claim we died that men might be fulfilled:
The earth should vomit us, against that shame.

We died: is that enough? Many died well
Of both sides: most of us died senselessly.
Ask soldiers who outlived us: they may tell
How many died to make men slaves, or free.

We died. None knew, few tried to guess just why.
No one knows now, on either side of the grave,
If you insist now, by all means try.
That being your trade, to make the knowledge save.

But never use, not as you honor sorrow,
Our murdered days to garnish your sorrow.

All the best to Ellen, see you in the spring perhaps.

I wrote that last line myself. Oh well, got to fly. I'll let you know how my visit with Eddie goes.

Take care,
Stephen

Suede or How I Stopped Worrying and Learnt to Love the Hype

Caitlin Moran

THE SEA, IMMACULATELY GREY, bends shallow and follows the flat beige curve of the shore. The few people crunching the pebble beach are tiny smudged black figures, mute, distant; framed by the white railings along the promenade. The wind comes running stupid from between the buildings, passes through your body, and carries on hurtling out to sea, occasionally taking a seagull by surprise and throwing it around in the air until the bird goes limp, drops towards the water, and at the last minute snaps open its wings and glides off into the faintly shining horizon.

This is Brighton. I was born here. There's an ace second-hand bookshop by the railway station, and – down the knee-shatteringly steep hill opposite – a shop devoted exclusively to selling foam rubber, cut to meet your requirements.

Today, all along the Sea Road, lies a coiling black queue of Kids, over three hundred of them, all smocked out in their different uniforms: Screaming Teenies, Glitter Queens, Glam Boys, Goths, slouching, stooping Indie Kids, a handful of The Dispossessed ™. Some of them sit slumped against the cinema

~~

wall that lines the street, playing poker and gin rummy. Others have turned the volume on their Walkmans right up, and are dancing to the faintly heard music. A couple are reading newspapers; the music press; battered paperbacks. Chewing gum, endlessly jerking yo-yos up and down, scuffing aimlessly at the wall with battered trainers and chewed-up Doc Martens . . .

It's four in the afternoon. The doors to the club don't open until 7.30pm. The band don't appear on stage until 10pm. Yeah yeah yeah; Suede are a music press invention and I claim my five pounds.

❖

Brett's sitting hunched up, his back against a rickety wooden chair backstage. There's a plate of sweet'n'sour tofu in front of him, which he occasionally stirs around with a fork. Bernard sits at the table on the left, resting his head on his hand, daintily picking over a salad, face hidden by a curtain of hair. Mat wanders between them, one hand in his jacket pocket, the other punctuating his conversation with a wave of a cigarette: *louche* and loquacious, a minor P.G. Wodehouse character perpetually ready for absinthe and tiffin or, failing that, a lagerfest.

'No, I want to be Lord Peter Dark,' Brett pouts, mushing his tofu.

'But you could be my trusty side-kick,' Mat offers. 'That's got much more room for character development. We could find hidden facets to your personality. You'd be much more rounded.'

'I thought of Lord Peter Dark. I want to be him,' Brett says petulantly.

'But you'll get all the totty,' Mat argues. 'Side-kicks get all the birds.'

'I don't want totty; I want an air of mystery,' Brett mock-sulks. 'I don't want to be your side-kick. Bernard can be your side-kick.'

Bernard looks up from his salad. 'Leave me out of this,' he grins.

'Oh honestly,' Mat says, walking towards the door, exasperated. 'I'll ask Simon. He'll do anything. He's a tart.'

Yeah yeah yeah; Suede are merely pop-theoreticians, just beautiful boys in tight trousers, pretty; *vacant*. Yaaawn.

❖

The stage is lashed with red and blue lights. Sweat drips from the ceiling, runs down the wall, drips down Brett's body as he stands for a minute in the spot-light. His essence-of-net-curtain blouse is ripped down the arm, slashed across the belly, stuck to his toast-rack ribs with damp. The venue is silent for a minute as Brett perches on tip-toes on the monitor, arms wrapped around his head, microphone lead tied to his wrist. All we can see of his face is his mouth; panting, gasping, blowing silent air bubbles. His hair is slicked and wet, clings to his head like a skull-cap. His body shakes with exhaustion and emotion put on hold for a minute.

A girl howls: '*Screw me now!*'

He grins, and the last chords of 'Animal Lover' crash back in, running and screaming for the finishing-line, snatching the air out of the audience's lungs. Bernard is whipping himself into a frenzy on the right, a psyched-out blur of peacock-blue shirt and desperately scrabbling hands. Mat is frugging himself stupid up against a bank of monitors. Simon has his head down on his chest, striking out at his kit, just an orange Bart Simpson hair-cut and two flailing arms. As soon as Security pull one fainting boy-girl thing out of the mosh-pit, another collapses and has to be rescued. A woman crushed by the bar is staring at the stage, eyes bulging, mouthing *'Fuck fuck fuck'*, endlessly. A boy is sitting by the toilet doors, crying and crying and crying. His friend is bent over him, torn between concern and standing up to watch the band. 'What's the matter?' he asks.

'They are – I can't – it's too – *Jeesus*,' the boy sobs. Song ends. A primordial vortex of noise, white noise, replaces Bernard's feedback; begging, celebrating, freaking out and ripping their throat-linings red. The audience is a carpet of pale arms in the air, applauding frantically. The screams of *'More!'* last seven minutes. Nothing more happens.

Suede don't do encores.

They don't need to.

Yeah, anaemic glam-rock rehash; the Bootleg Bowie, Smiths tribute, seventies on a loop going round and round and round, impostors impersonators *immaculate*: album in at number one, 'Top of the Pops', tickets like diamond-dust, front pages every week, *fuck you*. This band mean something. Everything. Anything you want them to.

❖

In the sub-literate years between the dislocated, bug-eyed trance-dance of Manchester and the mimsy, wispy diaspora of the thumb-sucking Shoe Gazer's Ball, this nation, one nation under a groove, was head-whacked-against-a-wall bored. The baggy lads liked to drink and liked to dance. List ends. Eyes smudged purple with exhaustion, they'd grunt through interviews, slope on stage and slope off again; peddling dope and E on the side: gangsters, a bit of rough and yeah, okay, occasionally a quick shag in an alleyway can be fun. Actually, a quick shag in an alleyway is *always* fun, but libido shouldn't get in the way of a good argument.

And my argument is with all those who disbelieve, all those who are cracking the whip for the Suede backlash. Picking faults with Suede is like having a downer on Christmas. Four bastard good-looking blokes who unfailingly get their round in; snort fire live; knock out slabs of The Gorgeous and The Great on all three formats; and, in interview, make Tallulah Bankhead look like J. Mascis. *Plus* they wear blouses. If Pop has become product, which it surely has, Suede are a trolley-dash around Tiffany's. *Breakfast at Tiffany's*. Christmas, at Tiffany's, with someone else's credit cards. And they're a special birthday treat with cream and biscuit on top for the Media – following on from the Manic Street Preachers' verbose mediawhorism, Suede made interviews a part of their art. Brett would spout darkly about sex and decay, punctuated by Mat either a) making a valid and salient point, or b) mercilessly taking the piss; whilst Bernard slumped in the corner and exercised his *ennui* by remaining silent, and occasionally shaping chords on his beer-bottle. In the early days of Suede's press blitzkrieg, journalists would come into the office, stand on a table and shout 'I've found a band who can talk!' until coaxed down by a kindly sub-editor or felled by a typewriter hurled by someone in Design.

For a generation utterly without heroes, Suede came at just the right time. 'If you're born in the suburbs, that's fine. But if you die there, you've lost,' Brett said in an early interview; and for young aspiring Julie Burchills and Paul Morleys, trapped in semis in Surbiton, with tube maps pinned to their walls, dreaming of the cruel wide streets of the City and the glamour and gloom therein, it was the truth. Manchester's finest seemed to revel in the fact that they lived in a grim town – the rain-soaked brickwork and air of recession were held up as something to aspire to. For a frightening, six-month spell, kids in Birmingham dreamed of leaving the Black Country to run away up to Manchester – Manchester! Basically Birmingham without the high standard of curry. Whoever ran away from home to seek their fortune in Oldham?

Dressing up for the night meant choosing from one of six hooded tops; and deciding whether to lace your trainers up right to the top, or leave them undone. Suede changed all that – four whippet-hipped boys in second-hand glory – daubed in Oxfam girl's blouses, shattered hipster cords and strings of beads strung round and around the neck: suddenly for under a tenner you could be your hero, walk around town planning how to get out, how to get away from the bland satisfied backwaters of small towns.

Suede canonised Dollis Hill and Tufnell Park and the seedy, violent end of Notting Hill. The big city was suddenly exciting again – the stops on a tube map read like lyrics. In a year, Suede did more for the image of London than half the musicals in the West End, and made the slums appear elegant again.

Brett's love of London's mythology is eye-poppingly obvious in his Notting Hill flat. The walls are plastered in old, tattered pictures of Bowie, ripped from colour supplements and magazines. Every available surface – from the top of the piano, crammed in next to the balcony, to the dangerously over-carved antique bookcase – is covered in Portobello Market finds and bits of glorious junk salvaged from jumble and car boot sales. When I first interviewed him there in Autumn 1992, he was already humming with the skin-coating stardom that seems to be Suede's trademark. He had that kind of Teflon self-absorption that usually comes with years of being well-known, and was quite willing to explain himself away for hours on end.

When did you first decide to be famous?

Probably at college . . . I would walk around in this lemon-yellow suit with my hair dyed blond, trying to be as fey and effeminate as I could. And obviously this annoyed a huge percentage of the lads there. They were nasty, harsh people – one person I knew had an argument with the gang there, and they put a metal bar between his legs and bent it around his crotch. Poor bugger had to go into hospital to have all the bits pulled back into his balls.

I think then I was working out a plan – how to get out. And it seemed dreadfully important to work out the details. All the things I adore about pop-stars rest on details: it's like their vision is so focused they can afford to fuss about the minutiae.

Where do you get your songs from? Some people believe their songs are part of them; others that they're from some kind of 'Inspirational Sub-Ether' . . .

It's this little demon racketing around in my head – it's been passed on through the generations and is strongest in me. My children won't have the demon, but their children's children will. And I'm glad that I have it. When the demon . . . actually I'm starting to wish I hadn't said 'demon'; it's starting to sound horribly twee . . . when – when I finally lose the ability to write songs I'll just fuck off and buy a farm and get out the way. There's nothing sorrier than seeing some ghost of a star being wheeled around the world, croaking out what he remembers of his set-list.

But while I am still fantastically talented and famous [*laughs*] I'm going to enjoy it. I've always wanted things to be like this. When we had that front cover [*Melody Maker*, April 1992] I couldn't get to sleep at night – I was so excited. I just walked around this room until four o'clock in the morning, going 'Yesssss.'

Why do you want to be famous? Is it to shag lots of young boy-girl things?

Obviously [*laughs*]. No, I think there's something very dubious about fucking your fans. I was trying to work out why I wanted to be famous. [*Long pause*] I do see my success as avenging my peasant stock, definitely. Being a pop-star is a short cut – you become aristocracy overnight.

First of all, everybody fancied you. Then for a short time it was Mat. Then Bernard – which I can understand: he looks so cool on stage . . .

Yeah, well, he's been practising in the mirror for years.

How does he fit in with the rest of the group? He seems very shy and intense, and you, Mat and Simon are so gregarious . . .

I think if you look at all truly great groups, there's that contrast between the two main songwriters. Lennon and

McCartney, Richards and Jagger, uh, those two guys in Abba probably argued about who was going out and who was staying in and stuff. I'm still stunned by some of the stuff Bernard comes up with. I think he's a genius. He said recently that he was a singer that couldn't sing; so he sang through his guitar. I thought that was very profound.

Okay then. Heavyweight question. What's love?

It's a really dreadful band from the seventies, isn't it? Um, love . . . it's this – *[Brett scoops his cat up and buries his head in it. He then starts sucking the fur down its back, very gently. You either find this horribly twee or unbearably cool. Me, I rather start hoping the album goes in at number one and stays there for a year.]*

Where do you eventually want to end up, and what do you want to be doing?

Married, kids, nice big house, lots of cats, lots of money. I want to be a truly, truly happy old man of seventy. And what will I be doing? I will be serene and at peace with myself.

However, once a year, on the anniversary of his death, I would like to go and jump up and down on Phil Collins' grave.

Another part of Suede's appeal is their DIY approach to fame – if you think you're a star: you are, instantly. Looking around at the audience at a typical Suede gig this ethos is something the fans have definitely picked up on – glitter-girls decked out in three generations' Sunday-best clothing; dolled up with Boots eyeliner and slashes of pillar-box red lipstick, wearing T-shirts much too small and lace-up boots way too large, strings of beads and haloes of patchouli oil. This, I would hazard a guess, is why Suede are so successful – to like them is to *be* like them, and to be like them is to be a star: self-aggrandising and fishing for something stellar.

So with a Number One album and a Mercury prize cluttering up their mantelpieces, it only remains to speculate on Suede's future. So far, America seems to be cautiously resistant to their pouting advances, but these things take time, as Morrissey is just finding out. Unless there is another huge shift in music opinion in the States, as happened with grunge, then Suede's future probably lies in being a very successful *alternative* band, rather than a mainstream act. From talking to people in the States, they're rather wary of Suede – having heard none of the records, but read all of the hype. With constant touring Suede *could* break through people's reservations – but that kind of intensive gigging takes years out of a band's life, and means less time spent in the studio writing new material. And less time having nice holidays and paddling those little lilo-things around in the sea. Suede will probably settle for a reasonable-sized whack of fame and a brace of spangly albums.

There were those who wrote Suede off, said they were just a pop thrill. *Just* a pop thrill – as if being pop isn't one of the greatest things in the world. And anyway, she said sniffily, Suede are a *deep* and *meaningful* pop thrill, and possibly the third greatest band in the world at the moment.

Most people would finish off by quoting an apposite Suede lyric here, but I feel that would be slightly tacky. So I've drawn a little picture of the band, instead.

In the Mind of the Bourgeois Reader

Thurston Moore

Part One

Waking up at 9 am in NYC can be a sexy thing. Especially when there's a female yelling up to your apartment from outside. I had to cut some overdubs that afternoon. It was our last day of recording and tomorrow at 3 we were moving studios and going into mix mode.

The morning was beautiful, sunny and cold and I knew right away whose voice it was. It belonged to this girl named Jennifer who was coming up to me at gigs to talk about music and stuff. She was always fawning but never really saying or doing anything embarrassing. For certain she was semi-voluptuous. And I knew she was cool cuz her name was the same as the girl from Royal Trux. Plus she was Jewish. I think.

She seemed to like me quite a bit and it was obvious it was only because I was an all-of-a-sudden famous 'alternative-rock' rock star. Not a stud, but a nerd. And therefore 'cool'.

Last night I had run into her at a free-jazz basement gig on Bond St. The underground tenor-legend Charles Gayle was playing and the atmosphere was very interesting. It was at this point that I knew something was going on, that maybe she wanted to make out with me or something, and I joked to her about how I'd love to get an early start the next day so I could get some personal shit done before running off to the studio. She asked me where I lived and I told her. She poked me in the hip and said, 'I'll wake you up.' And then spun around to socialize and hang out. I kinda really didn't know what to say but was excited and a bit nervous. As soon as the gig ended she split.

So that morning . . .

I bolted to the window with just my shorts on and said 'hey', and tossed her my keys in a sock. I threw a T-shirt on and started to make coffee. She brought a thing of orange juice with her.

Her first words were: 'Hey do you do drugs?'

'Um no not really.'

'I don't either,' she said.

'I mean I used to in school. Blotter acid was a big thing. But . . . you know, in New York it's too fucked. I'm kinda straight-edge I guess. I smoke pot once in a while . . .'

'Yeh, God, I love pot!'

'Really? Hmm, I might have something stashed away here somewhere . . .'

The thought of smoking pot with this girl was very exciting. That was indeed the situation where romance would almost have to be the outcome. And I knew I had a half-full one-hitter.

'You want some coffee?' I asked.

'Sure . . . here's some orange juice too. No, the reason I was asking was cuz my roommate broke up with this guy and he had left a tin-foil thing of cocaine in her bedroom. And um, it's been a while and she said she was gonna throw it out. Or I could take it if I wanted. She didn't seem to really care.'

'Wow.'

'Yeh so I thought we should do lines with our orange juice.'

'OK, but it's been a long time since I snorted cocaine. I don't wanna get a fucking heart attack or anything.'

'I think it's cool. She said she did some and it was pretty mellow.'

'Alright, let's fuckin' do it.'

She was laughing and I was super happy.

'You want milk in your coffee?'

'Yeh just milk.'

She had a razor blade inside the tin foil and chopped the shit up while I sipped coffee.

'How old are you?' I asked.

'21.'

'Hmmm . . .'

'You're 29 right?' She knew.

'Yep, I'm old.'

'Naw, but that's cool.'

She had on the dopest V-cut polyester-like thing – it was like a Burger King outfit but very luscious. Very rocking. We snorted the lines with a dollar bill and chugged OJ. It felt good almost immediately especially the OJ washing over the chemical taste. Smoking pot was the best chaser in the world for coke. And then when you start getting high on that you light up a cigarette. It's very amazing.

We were looking at each other just smiling as we simultaneously felt the rocking high.

'I'll get the weed,' I said.

'Yeah!'

I got the one-hitter and a lighter and sat back down.

'Here, you can have the first hit.'

I stuffed it for her and gave her the metal pipe.

'Hold it up so it doesn't spill.'

She wasn't hip to the one-hitter but that was cool cuz it was cute and she was right there in front of me. She took it all in and passed it back. As I was toking she sat on my lap and blew out smoke in my face. She was smiling all high and glass-eyed. We took a few more turns, put the shit down and then made out for a while.

'Hey, let's watch TV,' I said.

'OK.'

The TV was near the bed. The morning shows, to me, are a sublime turn-on – a vital part of the erotic effervescence of the chilly winter day.

And so then . . .

We jumped in bed and rolled around a bit kissing and petting. I pinned her shoulders down and straddled her waist kissing her face. Her hair was blonde with really dark roots. I pulled off the top of her Burger King outfit and started kissing HER VERY DELICIOUS, VERY SEXY BODY. I pulled off her skirt and her underwear and saw she had beautiful black pubic hair. I had sworn a long time ago not to obsess on any one body part and knew it was always much more rewarding to feel and sense the woman as a whole. Also I remembered reading something by a woman about how to totally approach giving head and one thing was to put in your mind that the girl is a queen you are servicing and you lick them as if you're invited into sacred territory. It's also much greater for the

man if he succeeds in this. Well that's certainly the head I got
into on that morning.

In the midst of my cunnilingus activity she would lift her
legs up and create a very penetrable position. I realized she
had come as she settled down, purring and laughing. I began
to lick her stomach but she got up and pushed me back. She
was stroking me and biting me and . . .

'Can we use a rubber?' she said.

'Yeah, of course.'

'Hold on.' She padded to her coat and came back with a
rubber. She put it on then straddled on top of me and began
to glide it in. She just moved around the head for a little bit
which got us both nuts and then slipped it all the way in. We
were fucking and while we were fucking she would arch her
back up for a while and then come down to me kissing me.
She turned around at one point and laid her back to my chest
and I bit her ear and neck while petting her whole body.
I was totally ready to blow it just then but I knew I didn't
want to and tried to slow things down. I slipped it out
in a way where I wouldn't explode. I cooled off for a little
and we lay side by side staring at each other. We started
to make out again and I got on top of her and slowly put
it back in and then we rolled onto our sides and gently
rocked.

'Where exactly do you live?' I asked in my luxurious
bed-tone.

'This girl Marcy has a place in Tribeca that I stay at.'

'She's your roommate?'

'Yeh, kind of.'

'I don't think I know her . . .'

'She works at A&M, she says she knows you.'

'Oh yeh . . . she's like a new A&R person there. She's cool . . .'

'Yeh, totally cool. She signed Snow.'

'Oh man . . . that's pretty heavy . . .'

'Should we do it doggy style?' she asked.

Amazing. I kind of froze. 'If you want, yeh.'

I only knew one other girl who liked doing it doggy style. You got to like to do it otherwise it doesn't really work. Jennifer was so hot doing it that I was gonna come instantly. Two strokes was the maximum and I had to freeze otherwise it was over. I told her this, my heart pounding, and carefully slipped out. She turned around and we both sat in the middle of the bed, me with a very much full on hard on. She began to FEEL ME UP and stroke my cock and I orgasmed like crazy.

'Whoa . . .' I sighed – she laughed and we fell back and hugged and scratched each other in the afterglow.

Part Two

'I should probably leave for the studio pretty soon.'

'You guys are pretty much done, right?'

'Yeh, it's just a couple of guitar things, all the vocals are done.'

'What's the cover?'

'Um, I don't know, I've had a few ideas . . .'

'John told me he heard some stuff and it was kind of minimal and maybe a little less crazy. He said he really liked it.'

'Oh yeah, that's cool. I'd play you something but I'm so burned on it right now.'

'That's all right.'

I was so in love with this girl. The cocaine was cheap and

the only remnant of it was wanting to smoke cigarettes. I wanted to ask her to come to the studio because I didn't want her to leave me. I imagined us staying in all day ordering food in, maybe doing a movie, and then spending the night and seeing where we were at the following day.

'I'm gonna call over there and see what's up,' I said.

'Yeh OK.'

'Do you have to go to work or something?'

'No, I'm going to school at NYU and today is like one class I can easily miss.'

I got through to our producer guy and asked him if he could find any other shit to do and let me finish later in the mixing studio. It was an outrageous request and I could sense him getting pissed. He was also curious as I'm usually pretty responsible and aware of what has to be done. I had to go in; I told him I'd explain later.

'You wanna go up with me?' I asked.

'Where is it exactly?'

'Up in the twenties on the west side, in Chelsea.'

'I should actually go out and buy a few things. I can call you there. Do you wanna see a movie or something?'

'Yeh, that'd be cool.' Movies were always cool.

'Did you see the Half Japanese movie?'

'Yeh, it's pretty funny. It's pretty good in a way. Gerard Cosloy actually disses Sonic Youth.'

'How radical.'

'Byron Coley is in it and Don Fleming and that whole gang.'

'Did you see Byron's thing on Charles in the last *Option*?'

'Yeh, he told me he hates *Option*.'

I had some more coffee and talked more about Half Japanese and movies and I got dressed to go uptown.

'I better run, you can leave when you want, the door'll lock behind you.'

'OK, good luck, try not to break any strings.'

We didn't hug, or do any horny stuff, or kiss, but it was cool and understood.

'I'll write a song about you,' I said, instantly embarrassed by the corniness of it. It was enough to create a dumb, awkward moment but Jennifer saved the day.

'I wrote one about you . . .' she said.

'Are you kidding?'

'No, I play with that girl Darlene from The Shadows.'

'Oh man, she's amazing.'

'I knew her from New Jersey.'

'You're from Jersey?'

'Yeah.'

'Hey, are you Jewish?'

'Yeh, why? You're not.'

'No. There's something really cool about certain Jewish people's eyes, and . . . I don't know . . . there's a really cool vibe . . . but . . . you know . . . it's a groovy thing . . . whatever . . .'

She jumped up to me and grabbed me kissing me on the lips.

'I'm gonna call Darlene and then go out.'

Part Three

Our band got big really quick. We'd been playing for five or six years together and were in other stupid bands before but for some reason our shit clicked. We signed after our first album came out on Sub Pop in '89. I had one girlfriend for two years and another for four. Each time I had been totally in love but both girls eventually got to a point where it seemed they were locked to a guy (me) and the fact that they could be locked there forever created a problem. Both of them, after we'd split, got involved with long affairs.

When MTV made us famous I started having sex with different girls and women. I had always aspired to have casual sex but I was too shy about getting it happening, plus I wasn't exactly Keanu Reeves. Most girls had boyfriends anyway. I figured on being a single loner guy for a while because usually every time I did sleep with someone I'd feel myself falling in unhinged love, forever again. I had to be careful.

She never called the studio and I was kind of bumming but I knew it wasn't a fluke. Our compatibility at gigs was a strong bond. But . . . you never know . . .

When I got home she was sitting on my stoop. She looked incredible with a pink pea-coat and an SOS Records knit cap on.

'What are you doing?' I asked.

'Hey, how'd it go?' she responded.

We went upstairs talking about record stores as Jennifer had made the rounds. She got a Bratmobile single, a Rudolph Grey CD, a Stereolab cassette thing, and a fanzine with a picture of me at a Hole gig. I wanted to hear the Rudolph thing as he was my favourite guitarist. It was pretty intense. She seemed to be genuinely into it which was interesting because most girls totally ignored Rudolph's more majestic qualities. And those qualities were very apparent on this CD.

'You know, I have to get this cover done for our album.'

'So, do it.'

'I had this idea of chopping up all these magazines and

putting together all the pieces like an abstract puzzle, but base it on colour and whatever else looks good.'

'That sounds pretty cool.'

'The thing is I should probably do it tonight.'

'You want me to help?'

'Yeh, if you want.'

'OK – we can order some food later.'

I wondered if she had any money. Most people didn't. I didn't until this year and now I'm fucking loaded. She knew that though, and that was cool. We listened to the Stereolab thing and sat on the floor cutting out squares and pictures from a ton of magazines I had. Her sensibility seemed very hip and unique and I was way into the stuff she was cutting out.

'What's Darlene up to?' I asked.

'Oh The Shadows are playing Maxwells with Skinned Teen.'

'Wow, that'll be hot.'

'Yeh, and Dame D'Arcy.'

'All right, D'Arcy. She lives around here somewhere.'

'Did you see that Nirvana's gonna be on Letterman?'

'Yeh, we're touring with those guys in April or something.'

'Oh my God, that'll be insane.'

'Yeh, I'm into it.'

'I heard they were booed in Chicago or something.'

'Yeh. I don't know man. They're nice guys but Kurt gets pissed at the playing situations or at shit they should've known going in. I don't know . . .'

'It's cool they're taking you on the road – who else is playing?'

'I don't know. Sonic Youth maybe . . .'

'Wow, that'd be intense.'

'Yeh, but we're too famous to go on first and Sonic Youth aren't gonna go on first either, so . . .'

'I heard Sonic Youth might do Lollapalooza.'

'I'd be very surprised. Sonic Youth with Lenny Kravitz and Johnny Cash.'

'They got a new record coming out.'

'It's done, I got a tape of it.'

'What's it like?'

'It's weird, I'm really into it. Eddie Vedder said he's really into it.'

'You and Eddie.'

'My good friend Eddie.'

'Let's hear it.'

This was bliss. I wanted to find out more about her band. Like if they even have a name. And I want to find out more about those girls who hang around The Shadows and what's up with them. I wanted to kiss her forever.

Thurston's lyrics were funny. Jennifer was at one with her work, bopping to the beat –

Seaside lover gonna rock the boat
Gonna roll it up fat superdope
Yeh pass it around or stick it on a pin
Boojie lover with the bunny skin
My plastic lady here's a glitter roll
Straight from my heart thru thy soul
Yeh I don't care about dirty hair
All praise due Queen and Yogi Bear
SAID GET BACK IN THE BOAT YEH!
Vicarious pleasure in my brain
Fantastic life never the same

Identity come set it free
Come set me out to mystery
MISTER E-MIND YEH!
Silly Rabbit trix are for kids
Yr carrot soufflé's got me on the skids
I don't care about dirty hair
Got a fuzzy finger miss bunny tail
HIP HOP TILL YOU DROP YEH!
HOP HOP HOP HOP HOP HOP HOP HOP HOP
HOP HOP HOP HOP HOP!

Stations of the Crass

Robert Newman

WE WERE TO LEARN A LOT about punk rock that fall on Walton's Mountain. I was sixteen and a punk, in a two-years-too-late, provincial way. Spikey hair. 'Destroy' T-shirt, distressed trousers.

Crass were the punk band of the hour. The NME described them as The Band Whose Name Is On The Back Of Every Black Leather Jacket – or, in my case, Brown Hooded Raincoat. Their songs were all one-minute spurts of speeding anarcho-agitprop three-chord thrash. The Godfathers of Crusty, they put out a 12″, 19-track, 45 rpm EP. *EP!* Bought this 'Feeding the 5,000' EP ('pay no more than £2.99') having never heard it, thought it was an album, played it at 33. Keen to be hip, I persuaded myself I liked it even at the wrong speed, and actually went to school the next day saying 'Oh there's this great band called Crass, they've got some fierce songs –', and then, like Lee 'Wandering Star' Marvin on low batteries, went about singing 'banned from the Roxy OK/ I never much liked playing there anyway.'

An ambition to be a music journalist was dealt a severe blow ❧

by the fact that the last train home to a village within walking distance of the village where I lived was at quarter past ten at night. So I used to go to all these punk gigs and have to leave after the first two songs. The night Crass played our local town hall, however, I wasn't sorry to do this.

There was always a lot of trouble between punks and skins in my home town. One banned skinhead gang had snuck in. With amphetamine grins they pulled on black Dexy's hats and wraparound shades: their tag. It said to the out-of-condition council bouncer: 'We're in now, and there's really nothing you can do.' As soon as Crass were three chords into their first song (that is, quite close to the end), a skinhead started jumping up and down on my shoulders, kneeing me in the back in time to the music. (Strictly speaking, I feel Sir Georg Solti would say that he was a little *before* the tempo.)

So there I am at 10.15 on a Saturday night; on a deserted railway platform waiting for the 'Titfield fucking Thunderbolt'. Bounding across the electric tracks laughing and staggering come punk Sack and these two skins. I know Sack from skateboarding, so I'm safe. He says he loves the new 'cold wave' and do I? Yeah, I say. Then I'm following them into the waiting-room. The two skins and Sack start sacking the station waiting-room, smashing it up, but in a matter-of-fact, almost absent-minded way. Crash, tinkle. The strip-light's extra bright now its casing's gone. Crash, tinkle. Dark again.

Someone had called the police, there was nowhere to run but chain-link, so I went and stood as far from the others as I could, and I tried to stand in an 'Actually, I'm doing three A-levels' kind of a way. Would've got away with it too, but then suddenly with 'the insolent logic of nightmare' one of the two skins chose that moment – just as the cops arrived – to come up and stand right next to me.

'All right, mate, how are you doing?' Cheery, friendly, he nodded towards the portly sergeant whom a small BR stationmaster was pointing towards us. 'Oops.'

So we all get arrested. And I'm struggling and saying to the sergeant: 'Oh please let me go, it wasn't me, please let me go, I'll get into terrible trouble at home.'

'All right. I'll let you go, if you tell me who it was, then.'

'All right, OK, I'll tell you. OK, I'll tell you.' [*Deep breath.*] 'It was all of them and not me.' We're all taken down to the station.

PC Stevens takes my statement. I'm refused charge which means I'm allowed to go without any charges being brought, on the grounds that I've liberally grassed up everyone I was arrested with.

When you're arrested as a minor they can't just let you go, you have to be collected by a parent/guardian.

'Hello, mum, can you come and pick me up? I've missed the last train . . . No, I can't walk, I've pulled a muscle in my leg.'

[*Much heavy tutting – so soon? Hold on a sec, the good bit's coming up, mother*.] 'Where will you be?' Oh dear. Ach.

'Ooo, let me see, I suppose you're coming through the Old Town . . . Tell you what, mum, what's the name of that big municipal building by the roundabout? Is it a fire station?'

'I don't know where you mean.'

'Hold on, I think I can see it from here – Po-lice St-ation.'

Then my mum gave one of those heavy sighs mums do: prophecies of the Accursed Spawn come true.

So I'm in the waiting-room by the desk sergeant, and

meanwhile Crass have been arrested. A punkette was getting beaten up in the mosh-pit, and Steve Ignorant – lead singer of Crass – had bravely jumped in, but ended up getting charged with an affray himself. We're in here together: out-laws on the edge of society.

My mum walks in to pick me up, looking that night like the poshest mum in the world, wearing a coat and matching handbag just-to-show-we're-not-part-of-the-criminal-classes, dear.

Picture the scene, dear reader, and pity me. There I am in all my punky gear, and I have to walk out past Crass behind my mum. Desperately, I tried one last half-hearted punky sneer, but I couldn't get it up. My country-lane credibility was in tatters, a return to skateboarding inevitable, when SUDDENLY – a door opened, and from out of the cold new-town night came my salvation: *in walked Crass's mums*.

As the day of the trial got nearer I thought, 'I can't go . . . The statement I've given drops everyone in it, and it's wrong to grass your friends . . . Even though strictly speaking these people aren't actually my friends, they're still very violent people . . .'

On the actual day of the trial I have a brainwave: 'I won't go.' Spent the whole day living in the corners of my eyes, dodging chance policemen.

It got to the end of the day . . . and nothing happened. Nothing happened the next day, or the next. And then one day, I turned the corner into the street where we lived, just in time to see a police car with a Detective Inspector in it pulling away. He'd been talking for an hour with my mum in the kitchen. What he'd said prompted one of those moments when an invisible hand taps the director of the film of your life on the shoulder, replacing him with another director who's got a much darker pitch.

Still didn't know that then. Turning that corner, with its friendlier chain-link, I was still on a roll. Even though it'd been pure fluke I'd missed the Inspector, I thought I was the Scarlet Pimpernel. As if I'd been in the kitchen with him and my mum the whole hour, wearing a scarlet frock-coat and a tri-cornered hat:

'Who knows where he can be this Robert Newman. He certainly seems a damned elusive fellow. Why, perchance he is not so very far away even as thou speak'st?!!'

An Inspector called, and what he'd said changes the whole complexion of the story. They'd been pegging the whole case on my statement – because I hadn't showed, Sack and the two skins had got off. But subsequently, one of the two skinheads had been murdered at Victoria Station, on the underground. And that wouldn't have happened, he'd said, if I'd gone and given my statement.

◆

In *Goodfellas*, De Niro says: 'Never rat on your friends, and always keep your mouth shut.' But if I had done, if I had gone to the courthouse, and just simply told what I had seen, told the truth, then maybe that skinhead would still be alive. (I'd be dead, but he'd, as I say, still be alive.)

I felt guilty about this for years. And it wasn't a guilt I could share with anyone. 'Cos everyone, say, knows what it's like to have grassed someone up and to wish they hadn't – a beating taken or whatever – but *no-one* knew what it was like to wish: 'Oh if *only* I'd grassed him up, then I wouldn't feel so guilty.'

I carried this intolerable burden of guilt around for years, all the time wishing: 'Oh if only I could have the time again, I'd definitely grass. If I could have one more chance.'

I have written this because I want the reader to understand exactly why it was that I did what I did on the night when, a few years later, I found myself in a pub in Birmingham, and I happened to overhear six Irishmen talking in what I took to be a suspicious manner; and why also, when I overheard four Irishmen talking similarly in a pub in Guildford, I wasted no time in going straight to the authorities.

Walking Around Being a Woman

Kristen Hersh

MY FATHER WAS A PATTI SMITH FAN before me, so my first impression was a very bad one. He used to play the *Easter* album in the house, and the title track freaked me out so bad that I used to plug my ears and run around in circles telling him to turn it off. 'Turn it off! Turn it off! Turn it off!' So he couldn't really hear it when it was on anyway: it was easier for him not to play it.

One day he sat me down and explained that there was nothing wrong with the record, and showed me the sleeve. I said something like: 'Oh no, it's evil, you can't have it in the house. It's just pure evil! How dare you take a word that means chocolate bunnies to me and scare me so bad with this!' But I was fascinated by the luscious armpits on the cover . . . that's the way I remember it anyway, Patti and her pits. I was probably about twelve years old. I thought: lesbians are *so cool*. Or *anybody* with pits like that. I just figured she *must* be a lesbian if she had hairy armpits. I probably should've looked at my parents' armpits, but I was too busy running away from their loud rock music – uurrgghhh, yucky! I liked my father's other stuff though, like The Doors and . . . well, I liked The Doors.

Soon I decided to give Patti a chance. This was just something that I *didn't get*. It started to sound good, I liked the sound of it, but I didn't know what the hell she was talking about. Twelve-year-olds don't really 'get' anything – they're not kids any more and they're not grown-ups either yet. All I got out of it was: cool pits, cool lesbian – which of course she didn't turn out to be.

It wasn't until I heard *Horses* that I thought: oh, *now* I get it. I was now a 'budding musician'. I used to listen to a tape of *Horses* and *Radio Ethiopia* while walking from my apartment in Boston to the studio, which was a three-hour walk. In the snow. So it meant I could listen to both records twice, every day, on the way to work. That's a lot of listening time to put in.

The only impression I really took away, the only word I could remember, was 'fingers'. But while I was listening to it, it was this whole planet. It's *her* planet. She made a whole world. She can bring you into her bubble of sound, but nobody else can, not even your own brain can. It's not *your* bubble, you can't grasp it and carry it around. Yet I remembered that she said the word '*fingers*', because she made it sound *so* beautiful and sleazy at the same time, and I couldn't figure out how you could just take a *digit* and do that with it . . .

My next peak experience with it was when my son Dylan was a baby – his favourite song was 'Redondo Beach'. When you're a young mother you really rely on music. Dylan had distinct opinions as a baby. I must've heard 'Redondo Beach' a thousand times, so I remember that one for obvious reasons.

Now, he likes 'Because the Night', although it could be 'The Boss''s version. I don't find that so odd.

In retrospect I realize I first heard Patti Smith out of context, and was very lucky that way. It was her bubble I heard. I didn't hear it as based in Seventies rock, or as coming out of a scene. I just heard a voice. It didn't seem so much of a 'fiery rebel' thing to me, and by the time I grew up I'd seen so many 'rebels' that it'd stopped meaning anything any more. I figured rebellion isn't really where it's at: it's been done so much.

In a way I also saw her as *so feminine*. She was so *delicate*, and her voice was so thin. It'd close up really tight like she was trying to squeeze the words out. She seemed kind of breakable, which is great. I mean, *that's* a planet!

All the references to Rimbaud and Genet and Burroughs went right over my head. My father had the poems, the *Babel* book and the rest. Poetry is great but it's always been so *quiet* for me. I like it as an instrument which she's very good at, but I'd rather hear her play it than have me stare at it.

When I worked with Lenny Kaye everyone assumed we'd be chatting about Patti. Well, *he* would. I would just have felt tacky doing it. But he'd always say: 'You're just like Patti. You two always go off on those tangents.' I'd think: oooh, I'm just like Patti! But then he'd say something like: 'And you do laundry just like Patti does.' So it was all . . . balanced out. Lenny's a great musician and the Patti Smith Group were such a different kind of band. He was such a rock guitar guy, and they'd 'jam', which is the opposite of Throwing Muses. It's interesting, but he couldn't explain or describe why they ended up sounding the way they did. Timing helped; the right place at the right time.

It'd be obnoxious for me to say I was any kind of kindred spirit to Patti. She did something great and colossally differ-ent, and I feel lucky to just jump in there every now and again. She *was* a first. I saw her as so physical, I like those physical things! I guess she was just walking around being a woman. She was so jumpy and screechy, and always going from confused/delicate to confused/screaming. We all do, of course. Maybe that's why men think of her as this anarchic rebel and women think: ooh, it's so pretty. Men are going WOAH! and women are going YAY!

If there *is* a parallel between us, maybe it's that she was dismissed as 'crazy' in the man-world of rock, and also dis-missed as a poet – like, she's not a real rocker, she's a poet, see. And therefore not so dangerous or strong. Too arty. That's hardly a basis for dismissal! She made an incredible mark, with dignity. She's a landmark, all by herself.

❖

To me, it seems perfectly natural to go from rock'n'roll to raising kids, but I don't know if I'm the best one to talk about that. To me they go together very well, except as far as *time* goes! Every day we have to make a decision to either work the record or take care of the children, so I can understand her wanting first to throw herself into a career that needs to take you body and soul, and then wanting later to throw herself into her children, something which needs the same kind of treatment.

I don't believe I ever did anything you could describe as 'fan-like'. At first I didn't know that she was still alive or any-thing! I felt as if I was digging up a dusty old book and falling in love with it. God, I hope I never have to tell her that!

Personally I like the people you'd call fans very very much and I'm aware they're the reason I can keep doing what I want to do. I feel very grateful to them overall. On the other hand I'm not so much shy as I am just a *private* person, so the idea of going out and trying to attract attention is totally foreign to me. I do feel uncomfortable with such things as signing autographs, because most famous people are pretty obnoxious.

I used to get very strange people coming up to me and *trying to be strange*. But the more well-known I got, the more they realized I was just a goofy dork and they shouldn't talk to me that way. Or else they just didn't like me any more and went off and listened to other bands. The people I meet now are very down-to-earth and usually don't begin any tortuous interpretations. They have as much right to an interpretation as I do: I'd never go: ppfff, it's *not* about *that*! I've got enough reviews doing that already.

Last night some kid gave me the first British piece written on Throwing Muses. He said it was his most prized possession but he thought I should have it. It was incredibly opulent, but *our* last quote was: 'We don't have any idea what the things written about us mean.' Especially the ones about sea-horses on roller skates. Our favourite was the one that said we were 'bad-assed rock'n'roll motherfuckers on a one-way ticket to hell and oblivion'. I'm going to live by that when I retire. I'll get T-shirts made up that say it. Rock hard; I ain't no poet!

I've never met Patti Smith. Our paths haven't crossed, yet. She lives in Detroit now, I think. Being a mother. So maybe we could hang out and bake a cake together. Not that I can cook. But we could *talk* about baking cakes . . .

Tonight, Your Hair Is Beautiful

Chris Roberts

POSSIBLY AS A DIRECT RESULT of giving rock'n'roll the best years of your life, you have a lousy memory. Still, you remember the first album you bought was *Ziggy Stardust*, closely followed by a second-hand *Bolan Boogie*. (You checked for scratches – you needn't have worried, it had *loads*.) Your dad chaperoned you to the record shop when you went to buy *Ziggy* with your saved-up money. Perhaps he thought you would otherwise be attacked by bisexuals in green trousers. When you bought your first single – 'Indiana Wants Me' by the enigmatic R. Dean Taylor – you were alone. Clutching the seven sleek inches of melodrama you felt like a catburglar, a jewel thief. This one had sirens on it and overt displays of yearning, and was on Tamla Motown, which had a cool reputation. When you found out that R. Dean Taylor was white, you were inexplicably crestfallen.

When Marc Bolan died in a car smash you pretended to be explicably distraught at school, milking the sympathy on the chance this might discourage boys from hitting you or encourage girls to kiss you. It did neither. Possibly, girls hit you. You don't recall.

Some time earlier you had gladly traded a perfectly good packet of biscuits for permission to watch 'Metal Guru', which had gone from number nine to number one, on 'Top of the Pops', on the school telly, so now, your grief was understood. Your dad brought you a cup of tea. You weren't, genuinely, very upset. After all, pop stars weren't real, they were from another planet. Sure, it annoyed you that there'd be no more T. Rex records, but it was so . . . *remote*. It was nothing to do with your life. That was the whole point. Pop stars suggested to you that there was a world beyond the hypnotic drabness of daily life at comprehensive school. It would be a realm of peak moments and glamour and fire and fantasy. It would not be suburbia, it would not involve bus stops or toilets or pudding. It would be full of flashbulbs and corks popping; it would be as loud as you wanted whenever you wanted and you would get to express yourself to enthralled appreciative throngs and discuss profound, um, *things* with bright sparky wizardlings. There would be lots of girls, who, you imagined enthusiastically, would combine the brazen sex appeal of Babs from Pan's People with the exotic mystique of, say, Cherry from Pan's People.

At this point, though it is embarrassing to reflect, you want keenly to be A Rock Star when you grow up – a sort of poetic, hip-wiggling crypto-messiah, both brainy and lusty. As you are only about the seventh best player in the football team, astronauts have to be old and walk silly, and firemen get hurt, you consider it the only course open to you. Your parents wince tolerantly, while ensuring you still do your homework. In hospital for a fortnight with a slightly surreal hernia, the only tablets you are interested in are the ones brought down from Wonderful Radio One by Johnny Walker which tell you whether Carl Douglas or The Osmonds are number one. This is also the only Johnny Walker you are interested in. You are truly young.

You buy an electric guitar from a man at the fairground, for twenty-five pounds. Clearly it has fallen off a lorry's back. And it's the colour of teabags. But hey, it's an Electric Guitar. You plug it in and it makes weird anti-social noises before you even touch it. Brilliant! You form a 'group' with an albino drummer, and 'play' in your parents' garage. You are matchlessly awful. Nine-minute versions of 'Jean Genie' – without the chorus, which has a funny chord in it – are not uncommon. Sometimes they unwittingly mutate into 'Blockbuster' by The Sweet. (These are the days when soap-on-a-rope, shoes with compasses in the soles and Hai Karate after-shave are serious commercial ventures.) Sometimes you just down tools and invent male bonding by talking about Jenny Hanley from 'Magpie' and Alexandra Bastedo from 'The Champions'. You are not markedly sophisticated.

So what you do is you go to college, which is what young people always do when not knowing what to do. You make the front of the local paper for getting into Cambridge, but this does not satisfy your craving for Rock Glory. Soon, you are to discover irony. Other sometime members of the 'group' go on to enjoy several chart hits and a feverishly loyal live following across the world. You would've gambled everything you had on this not happening. Conceivably, you did.

You are now down south, which is wild, crazy, decadent and bohemian (the way you see it), and a heap of fun. You read Baudelaire and Kerouac and Henry Miller and, y'know, all the guys, thus reaping the benefits of education – All

Human Endeavour Is Futile – but most of the time you read diddly squat. You pick up many bad habits. Nobody can accuse you of dilettantism because to this day you are rarely lucid without the twin props of drink and cigarette. Having met other young people who can gabble all night about art and films and Rock Music (not pop, *Rock*), you become rather excitable. You are even persuaded to dump your Genesis LPs – originally acquired because you were told they were deep, and you thought the artwork was ambitious and fantastical. Punk Rock happens. Like ninety-nine per cent of your generation, you are a half-hearted, lily-livered, fairweather, bogus, vaguely pathetic 'punk fan'. It is invigorating to see the pogoing crowds at the gigs but you don't like all the spitting and jostling and general dirtiness, even if it does facilitate the ludicrous belief that you are Living On The Edge. At a summer job at the fairground, where you hear Abba and The Bee Gees from 10am to 10pm, you sell T-shirts with 'Punk Rock' stamped on them to squaddies and girls with bad teeth. These are the third best seller, after 'Sod Off' and a picture of two pigs mating which bears the heading 'Makin' Bacon'. People buy these of their own free will.

Punk Rock is a catalyst. Back down south you unceremoniously and unforgivably jettison your bright, perceptive hometown sweetheart because you have, a week before your final exams, fallen madly in a cinderpath between love and lust with the singer in your latest pop (*pop*, not Rock) group. She is a blonde bombshell with a traffic-stopping laugh (the way you see it). This boosts your self-image. You co-habit for two years, share peroxide, get engaged, give each other presents then hell, cheat, break up, make up, break up, and somehow are still good friends fourteen years on. (You attend her wedding. You hear all about the divorce.) Your pop group, while it lasts, is a lame if ingenuous attempted facsimile of Blondie.

◆

BLONDIE were a group. And a phenomenon. They were Sort Of Punk Rock, and then they weren't. They reeked of *New York*, and to *naifs* like us that meant: hip, cool, sassy, nihilistic. It meant Andy Warhol and Dorothy Parker and Zelda Fitzgerald and Truman Capote and all the greats all jumbled up in a Mondrian's Broadway Boogie-Oogie-Oogie criss-cross of yellow cabs and 42nd St and Travis Bickle and CBGBs and Lou Reed and Patti Smith and Television and Mailer and Vidal. It meant: films, movies. Shades. It was the other side of the world and the other side of the coin. It was somewhere we could never hope to be.

We were quite content to accept that Blondie were 'punk' enough. We weren't that bothered or puritanical. Seemed like 'Rip Her to Shreds' and 'X Offender' paid sufficient lip service to all that 'threatening' stuff. Although Punk Rock was lively, it was also sadly life-*like*. Ordinary blokes got on telly. Stars were out. Flash was out. Grit was in. There were, apparently, no more heroes, and for a long time after this the 'scene' was dominated with all the dazzle of dishwater by anti-heroes, geezers, *sub-heroes*. (How could you aspire to being a sub-hero? What fun was there to be had in a world where airs and graces were devalued currency?)

Blondie were fronted by a star and no mistake. Not by a regular bloke, or chap, or fella. You would never bump into Debbie Harry down the pub, or in Sainsbury's. They say trust the tale not the teller, but in the best of Blondie the two were inseparable. She infused already great records with . . .

radiance? Panache? Aura? Beautiful baloney? Sure, they were plastic contrivances with No Soul Whatsoever (heart of glass? heart of *ice*), but even this was apropos to the apotheosis. The boys in the band were twenty per cent geeky, eighty per cent skinnily cool. Of course Chris Stein was to be envied with zeal. You could trace intricate layers of meaning in 'Poet's Problem' or 'Fanmail', or just marvel at the alchemy pervading the intro to 'Union City Blue'. Or the ineluctable thrills of Clem Burke's drumming. Even. Oh look, don't start me off.

They patented the Big! Exciting! video, and had plenty of zillion-sellers, like most of the tracks from *Plastic Letters*, *Parallel Lines*, *Eat to the Beat*, and *Auto-American*. They made me tingle. They made me go off to funny places in my head, although this does not in itself render them unique. I never saw Blondie play live. It didn't matter. The idea was great.

The funny thing is: I didn't fancy her. Well, when I say I didn't fancy her, I'm actually – what's the phrase I'm looking for here – *lying through my teeth*, that's it. Nevertheless, I don't believe it was *merely* that I fell in love with Debbie Harry's iconic image. I can understand why anyone would assume that – she was undeniably gorgeous and the 'Picture This' video, for one, made breathing a challenge – but I'm not just being wilfully perverse with hindsight when I claim that because everybody else lusted after her, I didn't. When all around me were losing their heads, and any vestige of dignity, I actually took perhaps priggish, perhaps prematurely politically correct, *offence* at any lewd or laddish comments hurled at her televisual presence. I felt protective. Possessive, almost. Here was a true stellar entity, worthy of my worship (not liberally granted unless there was, say, a Monday in the month) and a tough, snarling female role model to boot! Despite her playing up to some of the 'tartier' persona tricks (I quickly attributed this to a mischievous sense of humour – on this I was to be proven right), I didn't see her as a sexual fantasy so much as an aesthetic love object. Sounds rich, I know, but that well-known photograph of Ms Harry in a black Andy Warhol's Bad T-shirt was the crystallisation of my personal Keatsean beauty-is-truth period. I didn't dream of going to bed with her, although I'd be the worst kind of phoney New Man if I pretended now I'd have run a mile from the prospect. I dreamed, more often, of being *like* her. No man was that cool. Men were all blemishes, all huff and puff. Well, huff. I aspired to be that *glacial*, without emotion, beyond all passion and pain. Because I was not. Befuddled by too many dense and grave books too soon, too many fleeting stimuli, and the disturbing recent revelation that Love Hurts, I aspired to join the elite club of happy ghosts that were Warhol's '100 Marilyns'. My grasp on cultural chronology was almost as far out of whack as my grasp on modern mythology. Fickle as pop music itself, I'd swerved from reprehensibly wanting a trophy wife to resignedly wanting to *be* a Stepford Wife.

And to think that around this time somebody'd coined the phrase 'the blank generation'. I collected memorabilia. I got sillier and sillier. I knew the lyrics to 'Hanging on the Telephone' *in Italian*: 'Oh, non riesco a controllarmi! Non lasciarmi appesa al telefono! Attacca e corri da me!' (My exclamation marks, although it's a moot point.) I read *Making Tracks* – the *autobiography* – religiously, and lapped up such choice disclosures as: 'I was apparently a very beautiful baby.' I made myself respect Rosenquist and Johns and Oldenburg, although quite which hoops I Fosbury-flopped through to get there remains elusive. Most likely, from an elevated abstract/realist/ Third Wave viewpoint, I thought it was all *really cool*.

In 1980, Blondie's video for 'Atomic' featured Debbie Harry miming in a torn yellow 'Vulture' T-shirt and black bin-liner on a set designed to resemble the debris of a post-apocalyptic fall-out nightmare. But the key refrain of the song, which affected to be throwaway and shallow, was *'tonight, your hair is beautiful.'* I decided this was Perfection of the Form. The phoenix of romance rising from the ashes, or something. Hope through despair. I'd always thought pop music was a valid and vibrant art form. And a great crack. I clamoured for glamour. This was its Brahma.

❖

Dissolve to London. You are working in a record shop, which is the next thing young people always do when not knowing what to do, especially when they have an MA (Hons) degree in English. In commercial terms, Blondie are just past their peak. You are making an important executive decision, like whether to order in another fifty copies of 'Stand and Deliver' or another hundred. It's not your money so you plump for a hundred and fifty, plus a hundred 'Tainted Love' for good measure. (People bought singles back in those days.) You're a bit bored. A colleague tells you that yesterday Debbie Harry from Blondie officially opened the company's new head office in Kensington High Street, and traffic ground to a standstill across West London for four hours. Possibly the lily of the story is gilded, but hey, it's a good story. You chuckle. You finish another honest day's pretending to graft. Then you come over all wistful. Is it an entirely unrelated decision you make, soon afterwards, to pack in the job and sign on and do nothing whatsoever? Is it really?

❖

Blondie split. You don't know yet that Chris Stein is ill. Debbie Harry goes solo. She does some good stuff, but it's not the same. Sometimes she wears wigs and pulls funny faces. She appears sporadically in tolerable left-field films. You watch quietly from a (considerable) distance. What else are you doing? Sweet Fanny Adams. You have given up on your dreams of Rock Glory, that's for sure: what a puerile, lame-brain scheme *that* was. No more carting amplifiers around for you, no siree, you're way too smart. You're so smart you're watching telly all day, when you're not sleeping, or driving a decent compassionate girl up the wall with a snide cruelty staggering to you when you stop to think about it, which is rare. Well, it's her fault for not being *ideal*, isn't it? You are resigned. You empathise with Camus, and also anyone who's going down the pub with a fresh giro. You get a cash-in-hand afternoon job in a kitchenware shop fifty yards from your front door. Sometimes you even get there on time. You are sacked for shrieking 'Fuck off you fucking mad queen' to the gay manager. You are resigned. One Christmas your girlfriend rings you at your family's house and your dad says: 'Oh he's not here, I think he's gone out with that woman from Blondie.' You haven't really. He is making a joke.

Suddenly you are no longer a ropey version of Ray Milland in *The Lost Weekend*. Suddenly you are Hunter S. Thompson, or at least Lester Bangs (the way you see it). Abracadabra, you are writing for the weekly music papers, and like anyone who does this, you think at first that you are incredibly significant and influential. This boosts your self-image. You get into places free, get feedback on your florid outpourings such as 'That was wonderfully irreverent' or 'That was arrogant bollocks', get to be grotesquely indulgent, get off your arse and out of the house, and get to meet people, some of whom are girls. You experience gallows humour, honour amongst rogues, and a nagging sense that you are indeed, as the cliché goes, a parasite. Still, you tell yourself, better me than some deaf schmuck with no good gags. Best of all, you get to travel, abroad, expenses paid, swanky hotels, new horizons, New York . . . *New York*! On your first day there you walk along Broadway with Tom Waits during Hurricane Gloria. You see yellow cabs. You *touch* yellow cabs. You see the sights. In this job, you don't even have to soundcheck. The only down-side is you have to hang out with rock stars. On the other hand, you get to hang out with rock stars. These creatures are either glorious or gormless. Increasingly, the latter. Of course you realise that all taste in music is subjective, but swift development of an overweening sense of self-importance allows you to ignore this. It also helps you deny assimilation of the fact that you are not a poetic hip-wiggling crypto-messiah, both brainy and lusty. Not as such. You are Boswell for bozos. You are Wogan for whey-faced wastrels. You are next week's cat litter. It sure beats the kitchenware shop.

Along the line you hit on the notion of a Blonde Movement. It just falls into place. A handful of buzzing bands with blonde singers are disputably fashionable. You find them very entertaining indeed, not least because of their sonic/visual resemblance to the unforgettable Blondie. Fat on a diet of Mailer's 'white negro' cant and Lichtenstein's hidden shallows, you concoct elaborate manifestos and philosophies stressing the cultural weight of these outfits, interpreting their each and every grin or chuckle as a semiotic earthquake. You borrow the dafter bits of Tristan Tzara, which is going it a bit on the daft front. You battle against 'Blondism' – *blondes are not dumb!* This one runs and runs, probably for somewhere between fourteen and sixteen minutes, with yourself cast as a mock Blonde svengali. The neo-tragedy is that people miss the comedy (spoof) aspect, which is like failing to notice a double-decker bus in your bathroom. You will be forever painted as the bloke with the thing about blonde bands, your hundreds of 'loftier' causes seemingly forgotten. Poor you. It is essential that something else happens.

Then something else happens. While accepting that nine out of ten heroes prefer to be disappointing simpletons, you have, in your line of work, been given a banana by James Brown, the Godfather of Soul, stared at a plant (to see if it did anything 'sexy') with Barry White, been professionally charmed and brought up to date on Russian politics by David Bowie, saved Iggy Pop from walking under a car and seen him turn up at your birthday party, presented Patti Smith with copies of *Under Milk Wood* and *The Wasteland*, and been completely forgotten by Al Green, who pops out 'for five minutes' for forty minutes. It's highly unlikely, however, that you will ever get to meet Debbie Harry, isn't it now?

❖

You are on your way to New York with the express purpose of meeting Debbie Harry. You're to interview her about her 1989 comeback tour and album *Def Dumb and Blonde* and you are being *paid* to do this. Jaded by the sallow calculations and dull common sense of the music industry's star-making machinery, you embrace this (last?) opportunity to be a head-long unadulterated unapologetic wide-eyed *fan*. Maybe you even overdo it a little.

You are in Howard Johnson's on Times Square and you cannot chew your lunch. An experienced, consummate trooper: are you perhaps just a tiny bit nervous? You are a whale-sized bit nervous. Slightly jet-lagged (a convenient excuse), the only eerily soothing parallels you can draw with the lion's mouth you are just about to headbutt are 1066, the storming of the Bastille, and maybe Halley's comet. It's destiny or nemesis. Springing about the hotel room, staring at the mirror, you make a snap decision to shave in forty seconds, having earlier plumped unswervingly for the rugged unshaven look. Dashing through unfamiliar shops, the only shaving foam you can find is called 'Beardbuster'. This is not a good omen and you botch it badly. After all these years planning What You Would Look Like When The Moment Came, you look like Lee Marvin if Lee Marvin were indecisive. And a mule in a snowstorm. You curse. You set off. The Chelsea area gleams in smoky sunlight. You pass Telly Savalas in the street. *You pass Kojak in the street*. Is this supposed to put you at ease?

On West 23rd and 9th is the Moonstruck café, where you're to meet at 4pm. You choose a table (much deliberation) and stare at the formica for seventeen minutes. You check seventeen times that your tape recorder is working. You chant Nietzsche's maxim that that which does not kill us makes us stronger. You grumble that Nietzsche never had to meet Debbie Harry. You tell yourself you are just going to do a sensible job of work, but your inner child, with whom you are in uncomfortably close contact, seeks some kind of epiphany today. Your inner child has waited a long time for your outer shell to do something this interesting out in the real world.

At 4.17pm Deborah Harry, as she has taken to calling herself, walks in wearing mirror shades with tortoiseshell frames and *lots* of blonde hair. It is definitely her. You stand up and signal that you are possibly you. Handshakes, nervous chuckles from both parties. She orders iced tea and immediately two of the staff ask for her autograph. 'I asked them to do that', she says with a throaty, loopy, jingle bells laugh. The two of you throw non sequiturs back and forth for ninety minutes. It's only surreal when you allow yourself to admit it. She is likeable and self-deprecating and only appears slightly scatty to you because you are looking for a guru to make sense of how you got here. You are hindered by the impotence of being earnest. It's you that's mental. It's you that's a casualty of too much rock'n'roll fantasy. She's just fine.

❖

'That's sweet', she says. 'It's like when you look at a drawing and put your own imagination on it and say, "Oh, this is *this*." It's like believing in a saint; it's like mythology. You envisage it as being so wonderful to be like them, but you have no idea what the person is really like and what their life is like. It has nothing to do with reality.

'I'm just a *schlepper*, y'know? I'm just doggin' around like everybody else, it's the same deal. Ha! I don't really enjoy that people go through that phase as kids when they're insecure and unsure of themselves. I certainly went through that – pop stars were the ultimate people, and had so many good things. Well some of them do and some of them don't. Some people make good decisions and some bad, whatever business they're in. If you're entertained by something, if it takes you away and makes you feel good, that's really what counts, that's what it's for, right?

'That's so deep, ha! Let's go on to . . . weightlifting. I don't know anything; I'm an idiot, y'know? All I do is walk around thinking "Woah, my God!" Let's get back to Earth now! I thought it was sorta cool we should come here. *Moonstruck*.'

Did you like the movie? (I don't miss a beat).

'I actually *did*. I liked some of the philosophy. Y'know, when Nicolas Cage said that business about: *love is a really horrible thing*. I thought: this is kinda profound, I like this.'

I miss a beat. Are you vain?

'Huh? Oh sure. Well, I'd *better* be. It's under control, in that I'm not scalping people or doing weird things. But it's good for me, it works for me. Anonymity is a nice thing but I mean *it's not my job*. It was a funny thing being a girl singer during the punk era. It was an odd position to take. Since I was a front for a bunch of guys it was like some of their perspective came through me, so I couldn't be "real cute". I *was* cute, but I had to be tough too. So that helped me in a way. It made me become . . . uh . . . *schizophrenic*. Yeah, ha, that's it.'

I thought 'Atomic' was very profound. I know 'make it tonight, oh, your hair is beautiful, oh, tonight, tonight' made me want to put an end to nuclear warfare singlehandedly. And maybe sort out anything else that was bothering anyone, anywhere, at all.

'Ah. Well it is a political song. Actually. Yeah.'

But also it's a song about hair, *beautiful* hair . . . do you see what I mean?

'Whoops! Ha ha ha!'

I don't know why she says, Whoops! I don't think *she* does. Whatever, we're laughing like hyaenas on helium. *Is there an option?*

We're onto *Dangerous Liaisons*, and then the citric sitcom 'Married With Children', which I hazard will put people off marriage.

'I suppose. Most people are off it anyway, aren't they? Are *you* married?'

NO! I mean, no.

'Do you *wanna* get married?'

Implausibly, I again answer in the negative. I may experience trouble coming to terms with that response for the rest of my life. At least I manage: you?

'Mmm, no, I'm not looking to get married, although I can't say that I wouldn't ever do it. Have to find out what the statistics are.'

It's a very romantic idea.

'Yes, it's nice. I still think it's a nice thing. It's nice to have a ceremony, I think.'

But the moment I was undoubtedly born for has passed. Did I leap panther-like upon it, guzzle its blood voraciously? Did I hell. I did a fair impression of a fridge magnet, four of which I give her along with a postcard saying: 'The point is not to put poetry at the disposal of the revolution but to put the revolution at the disposal of poetry'. I mean, I just *know* she'll understand.

'You're held by yourself, y'know? You can never escape yourself. It's as simple as that. Oh – I can't believe it, the time went really fast, didn't it? I have to go, we have our first rehearsal with the drummer. Do you think you have enough stuff?'

I guess so. I mean no. I mean basically I'm just keeping you here as long as I possibly can.

❖

As you leave the café you prevent Deborah Harry from tripping over a dog.

❖

'I was Warhol's favourite pop star?'

Sure, it's a well-known aphorism.

'Yeah, I don't know . . .'

There's a hint of schoolgirl mischief as she reaches for her shades. 'I'm *my* favourite pop star!'

That makes three of us.

❖

You walk away, completely dazed. You walk in circles. Actually, you walk the streets of Manhattan, so, more probably, you walk in squares. You think 'I am walking the *mean streets*', but they can seldom have been so generous. You have broken bread (the way you see it) with a walking piece of pop art history; you have crossed paths, you have breathed the rarefied air. You are *in that world*.

Though you are undeniably old enough to be less impressionable, you are young enough to not want to be. You are thrilled to bits. New York is your kinda town.

❖

A mere twenty days later come seven days that shook the world. Deborah Harry visits London to play a week of shows – a week-long magnificent celebration of The Pop Star – at the Borderline, a happily intimate club off Charing Cross Road. You've never seen her play live before so you go *every single night*, to make amends and do joyous penance. You are as much heart-in-mouth as tongue-in-cheek. You are a born-again *fanatic* (dictionary definition: filled with abnormal enthusiasm). You are all dressed up with somewhere to go. Intense scrutiny of The World Today tells you that this makes as much sense as anything else. This week you get called many things, among them 'adolescent', 'a sick man', and 'me old mate good to see you fancy a drink reckon you could introduce me?' You are . . . (*adopt movie trailer voice*) *relentless*.

Outside, people offer ludicrous sums of money for tickets. Yours says: Number 001. You're not selling. Monday, the opening night, you are beside yourself. Fortunately for your horizontal hold, also beside yourself is a young lady who declares she's never seen you so happy, then adds: 'It's Christmas!' Then she wonders aloud if God can smile like Debbie can. The Great One is resplendent in scarlet dress and gold crucifix, sighing 'The Hunter Gets Captured by the Game'. Well *yes*. You are dumbstruck. Tuesday night, for some reason – it's feasible that you are inebriated – you approach Samantha Fox and ask her opinion. 'Fantastic!' she comments. 'She's my idol!' Encouraged by this, you inquire if she cares for the new material as much as the classics. 'Fantastic!' she remarks. 'She's my idol!' Sam is now in her fourth term at your academy of objective music criticism and is one of your most promising pupils.

On Wednesday Deborah starts a rant about 'tough chick stuff. You wanna know what tough means?' Then she forgets what she's saying. 'The *Sun* was right,' interjects Chris Stein. 'Her mind is gone.' It is not alone.

Your escort this evening is – attentive readers will appreciate this – our old friend the blonde bombshell with the traffic-stopping laugh (the way you see it). 'Hhhmmm', she observes. The next night you nag her into accompanying you to a party. It is essential that you take a girl with you, so that you don't appear too sad or desperate, but equally essential that it is not any girl you are involved with or who might harbour illusions that you are an adequate or mature human being. She comes along, but – you break into applause at the recollection – wears a jet-black wig.

On Monday, you see, shortly after you told Alannah Currie that you weren't too keen on The Thompson Twins and that your dad was a deadringer for Harry Dean Stanton, the latter remark being appropriate because of Ms Currie's pithy lyric to 'I Want That Man' (the Deborah Harry comeback single), she invited you to a party. Her combo's album launch, or somesuch. You don't recall. You have an ulterior motive which is approximately as subtle as sandpaper.

Thursday, you attend, convinced you are glowing with an elegance that would shame Grace Kelly. You pace yourself, outlast the fairweather fans, and have a conversation with La Harry. Then another one. Then – oh fancy you standing there – another one. You are on such a roll that you forget to make a svelte exit from the party until the good Alannah tells you to, and you quote, 'Fuck off now'. But nothing, *nothing*, can hurt you, because you have told Debbie about this melting sensation, and because she has promised to dedicate '(Always Touched By Your) Presence Dear' to you. At least you *think* she has. You can't say for certain because 'for certain' is three syllables. Also you have a mental age of six this week, and as a fan know no dignity and therefore no shame.

Friday, metaphysical theories of Debbiedom abound. You are lectured and lampooned and licensed and loving it. The right side of your brain places bets with the left side as to how long it'll be before someone uses the word 'uncanny' again. It's, on average, eighty seconds. This number reminds you of how many drinks you enjoy that night. (People bought drinks back in those days.) Tanya Donelly (then of Throwing Muses, now of Belly) opines, 'That face is larger than life. That face *goes on forever.*' Your cab driver (musical background not established) says, 'Oh yeah, I remember her. Marvellous. These Sonia and that, y'know, they haven't got it, they don't impress . . .'

'That's right!' you yell, bouncing up and down because the cab driver is not only your best friend in the whole world but also a visionary poet. 'They don't *impress!*'

Saturday, Bette Davis dies. Things get better after that. You ask for the moon because you have the stars, and throw away your seatbelt because you're in for a bumpy night. Someone throws a bunch of red roses at Debbie. She bites the head off one and spits it out. You feel . . . unstable. After the gig you go for a nightcap with some chums. You've been there ten minutes when in swans . . . you know who. You act dead cool (wave ferociously, beckon, shout) and Deborah and friends join your table. Then, with a murderous smile, she gives you the red rose she's carrying. This is all so very very unexpected that you manage to keep it together for a half-hour conversation about Monet or Manet or some such painter bloke. She tells you (after some prompting) that she's been *meaning* to dedicate 'Presence Dear' to you, but the drummer keeps starting it the second 'Brite Side' finishes.

Yeah *sure*, you say, but what's my name?

'Uuuhh . . . Marty Wilde??'

By now you are the most hated person in the bar, in the West End, in the world as you recognise it, and it is entirely delicious. You revel. In fact someone brazenly steals your rose at one point. You catch them and they realise they have a simple choice between returning the rose and certain death. You sneer at their limp capitulation.

You stagger home with your magic rose. Debbie Harry gave you a red rose. The grail. Baptised. Sanctified. They can laugh. *But not as much as you.*

That night, you sleep like a baby, with whooping cough, on a spacehopper.

Sunday night: the finale. You make sure you are standing alone, lost in the crowd at the front. You don't want to talk to anyone tonight. You must memorise, relish, savour. You can't help noticing that Kim Wilde, daughter of Marty, is grooving daintily nearby, but by now absurd coincidences and surreal juxtapositions are meat and drink to you. The encore is pumping away and then what happens is this.

'This one's for Chris if you're here. I'd like to sing this one for you.'

If you're here?? Whatever, you beam and beam and beam. The culmination of a dream. Admittedly, you've cajoled and hassled and put the hours in for it (by now the Chrysalis press office think of you as a kind of low-rent Mark Chapman), but you respect your clarity of purpose, your tenacity, your fulfilling of an existential mission. This boosts your self-image. '(Always Touched By Your) Presence Dear', while it lasts, transports your corporeal form (highly motivated kamikaze jelly) to a state of grace. You could lick your spine with pride. You don't look for your friends in the audience to check they heard, nor do you want to crow and brag (until the next day). A red rose and a dedication. And tolerant pecks on the cheek are now standard. Bit of a result. Only a complete clown would ask more of their chosen idol than that.

Your middle name is Coco.

◇

Oh, there's more. You won't let it lie. From this plateau the Deborah Harry comeback comes back, and forth, with varying degrees of success. Naturally you attend all the London dates, and one in Brighton, or Bristol, you don't recall. You do miss *one*, being out of the country. Hard-to-get, that's you. It's probably just as well. Otherwise people might accuse you of being a self-parody or something.

Occasionally you exchange pleasantries with the *Diva Assoluta*. You present a calm, hopefully wry and ironic, surface, but each time you still have to pinch yourself afterwards. You run each sentence spoken through your head, analysing it for subliminal messages, for suggestion and code. Then again you tend to do this after buying a pint of milk from the corner shop. So maybe all this Debbie Harry stuff doesn't betray any psychological abnormality whatsoever.

Then: a pinnacle, from where there is nowhere to go but somewhere else. After this, a voice in your head tells the fan in you to count your blessings, call it a wrap, rest on your laurels, *give it a rest*, perhaps even 'grow up'. Again.

You have been Mister Shallowhead at a highly enjoyable Saturday night Brixton Academy show, and with irrepressible conviviality are imbibing to excess at the post-gig lig thing upstairs. It is late. Someone covertly mentions that Queen Deborah is going on to The Fridge (a nearby club).

Fridge-magnet, you free-associate. Because this has been mentioned covertly, you – with the gullible zeal of the truly pissed – consider it *imperative* that you're there. Once more after the forbidden, the denied, the utterly unattainable, the pointless. You bully two weary, only semi-interested friends into coming along, and skilfully navigate the eighty-five yards or so to The Fridge. Next thing you know you're inside – conceivably, you even paid – and, having bought your understandably impatient companions overpriced cans of soothing nectar, you are casing the joint, a driven man. The kind of driven man you *should* be around now is the kind that sits placidly in a taxi and gets taken home to collapse, perchance to dream. But this is not your agenda. You are on your Debbie Harry quest again. *It is something you do from time to time*. You have no choice in the matter. Some go fishing. Some climb Everest. Others get religion. This night is to be your last fully-fledged and sincere death-or-glory Debbie Harry quest, though you do not know this as you lift off.

Your reconnaisance is successful. She is in some kind of VIP bar, off to the side. You go back to your friends, who are standing near the dancefloor. A light-bulb goes on inside your skull. Attempting to groove, you say, 'I am going to ask her to dance.' Your friends are duly sceptical. Like: *as if* you're going to return with *Debbie Harry* in tow.

You return with Debbie Harry in tow. You have been decisive. You have grinned and said, 'Would you like to dance?' Simple as that. She has looked unnerved for a moment, conferred with the omnipresent Alannah, then said, 'Okay, sure.' Simple as that. Agreed, it's hardly *Les Amants du Pont-Neuf*, but you're thinking: as time goes fucking *by*, pal.

Moving towards the dancefloor with Debbie Harry, it is possible, you moron, that you are strutting. You realise *now* that you are carrying a can of Foster's lager in your left hand. (Well your *fag's* in your right, isn't it?) You must lose the can. *Lose the can!* Brain to hand: *lose the can!* You are presently a flushed, sweaty and hopelessly pissed lout from the nether regions, so it's fascinating that you feel you will not be suitably chic and Gatsby-like unless you lose the can. You push it into your friend's hand as you pass. 'If you only do one thing for me ever', you hiss importantly, '*hold my beer now!*'

The living legend and you find yourselves mid-throng, shuffling gamely to '(I Got) The Power' by Snap. It is not a record you particularly care for but you are not about to express your reservations. You concentrate on not falling over. No you don't; you are too drunk and elated to worry about shit like that. You imagine you are dancing quite well. You're a touch confused when she suggests getting up on the stage to dance, but follow obediently. In for a penny. Sheep as a lamb. Might as well make a prat of yourself up there as down here. Fortunately the bouncer will not allow even The Queen of Pop to clamber onstage at this time. You're secretly relieved. 'Oh well', you shrug articulately.

The beat goes on. You carry on dancing, blanking out all nerves with zen fortitude. Your self-consciousness goes into denial. Boom, chick, boom boom chick. Easy-peasy. The next thing that happens is she puts her arms around your waist. You put yours around hers. Well, you're not *stupid*. You know the routine. You sway together.

What you're thinking is: nothing at all. What everyone else is thinking, probably, is: poor old Debbie Harry, having to humour saddo fans like that all the time. *And* he's pissed.

You look at the face of the woman you're dancing with, a face you've eulogised for over a decade, and she looks great and you smile and she smiles. You sway together. It is all very innocent. You are happy.

'I better go', she says after a couple of songs. She says this suddenly, and points at something. She walks in that direction. You follow. She goes into the ladies'. You don't follow. You have presence of mind.

You hang around a bit, with no plan. You light a fag. Then you feel like getting your can of lager back. You drink heartily and narrate every nanosecond of your bop, your adventure. All things are possible. If you wish for something hard enough it will happen. Especially if you're as obnoxiously pushy as all-get-out.

'Can we go home now?' your friends plead, sated with sur- realism. Yes, but first you must say goodbye. You find her back at the table with her friends. You wave vapidly. She waves distractedly, as if through a mist. It belatedly dawns on you that she is as off her face as you are. But what a face to be off, you chuckle inwardly, as, far from crestfallen, you euphorically regale your companions with finely observed detail all the way home. You got the power.

❖

Pages fall off calendars. Seasons pass. Behind some indiscern- ible twitch of the clock you transfer your imaginative energies onto other targets, other victims, other monuments, other projections. Are you finally, *finally*, 'growing up' again? Not as such. You leave your rewarding job to make pop music again. Are you retarded or something? After all you've learned, and as an alleged music biz insider, are you really dumb enough to jump down that manhole? Try stopping you.

You don't of course get to be on telly, but it's an engaging spell. You release records which earn a modicum of begrudging respect and no-one throws squashy tomatoes at you. Sure, you miss the acclaim and adulation of being someone who just stands there and watches, but there are cheering moments, if not cheering multitudes. Nigel Harrison, formerly of the pop group Blondie, is in the audience one night. He says he loved it. You say 'Thanks' and act all busy and preoccupied, partly because it's just too weird and partly because you are an arrogant fool.

One wintry afternoon you are at the offices of your record company chatting and a woman walks into the room.

You are miles away, but think: I know her from somewhere. 'Hi!' she smiles. You recognise her now. You are as stunned by the crass and paltry symbolism of your not having recognised her instantly as you are by the fact that she's just walked in. It's *her*. She asks how your band's going and everything. You proudly dig records and tapes out of the cupboards and give her presents. All your own work. Something you made. You ask what she's up to. It's like two artists, or two salesmen, idly chewing the fat. You feel quite comfortable, you really do. Outside the window the sky darkens. You ask how long she's in London and invite her to your group's gig the following week. She says she'd love to come. Then she goes to meet the person she came to meet. Bye, nice seeing you again. Take care. Yeah, good luck with it all.

❖

When the wonderful people in your wonderful group are grumping about trivial matters such as not getting paid, not being filmed by Martin Scorsese, not getting to sleep with Linda Evangelista and so on, you will say anything to appease them and raise morale. 'Debbie Harry's coming to the gig on Tuesday', you announce at a rehearsal. You are wisely pessimistic yourself, but reckon if she made it, that'd be good. You play the gig. It goes fine. Debbie Harry isn't there. Since you are not selling millions of records and being hailed as a *fin-de-siècle* rock god or even a poetic, hip-wiggling crypto-messiah, both brainy and lusty, anyway, you have learned to be philosophical about life's arbitrary bouquets and brickbats. And so you are philosophical about this.

You haven't bumped into Debbie Harry since. When people tell you anecdotes concerning her (everyone still assumes you are obsessed), you are politely attentive, but detached. You had a teenage crush on Debbie Harry that lasted longer than any flame in 'real' life, because she was always on the pedestal. She wasn't flesh and blood. She couldn't answer back. She didn't have a three-dimensional personality. And then she did. And she was great, and funny, and bright, and friendly. She wasn't a cipher, or a silk-screen, or a muppet, or a goddess. She was who she was. And then you weren't infatuated. You actually *liked* the woman.

❖

'We're going to do "Cautious Lip", the Blondie song', your girlfriend at this time tells you. She is a singer, is from New York, and is often keener to watch 'The Complete Picture' video in its entirety than you are. 'I don't think that's a good idea', you say. She is initially annoyed. 'I don't think you should do cover versions', you say. 'Your own songs are great.'

You are the practical, supportive type. She does the song anyway. You feel ambivalent the first time, then after that you just enjoy it.

❖

You also enjoy – despite concerted efforts to attain maturity – the sight (and scent) of flowers awaiting you at soundchecks. And letters, poems, occasionally books. You would like to think you enjoy all this with a healthy dose of irony, but the truth is you just plain enjoy it. You are bewildered at the quantity of Rimbaud collections you are given. To your eternal shame you catch yourself quipping, 'I'd've preferred money.' It is immediately clear to you why the vast majority of rock bands are dull and tedious people. You tire of the apathetic response to your *cri de coeur*. You can't enjoy being small-time. A microcosm won't nurture narcissism. Like so many grand schemes designed to rattle the map, this one of yours starts to just sort of fizzle out. (Although to this day get a drink down your neck and you'll cite how ahead of your time and misunderstood you were till the catalogue numbers run red, etc. etc., yawn.) During a period of weakness and self-doubt you go out with someone who only knows you as this persona, who knows all the lyrics backwards, who you can persuade yourself is a *fan*. This boosts your self-image. She dumps you. This doesn't. You get to number two in Switzerland. This boosts your image of Switzerland.

❖

You do not revere pop stars any more, because you know they are just as brilliant or banal or erotic or neurotic as the next-door neighbours. You like and admire some. Their courage, their style. Others genuinely distress you. Their petty whingeing and grudges; their egocentric inability to see The Big Picture. If you'd never seen the intestines, the How It Works, you might still be able to suspend disbelief the way you can, gladly, for dead people like Marvin Gaye, the insurpassably funky Bolan, or Maria Callas. Or a fine actor or actress, or writer, or ballerina, or Wimbledon champion, even if they don't have cool hair. (Though it helps.) The thrill isn't gone, but it's a thrill of your own devising. It's up to you when you switch it on. The romance, sparks and inspiration happen on the bridge between fickle fantasy and rigorous reality. It's up to you when you take it to the bridge, and sigh.

You still throw yourself into great records; they nourish and bolster you. Indeed you are currently recording the album of the nineties (the way you see it). You still clock the shock of the new: you're such a hip-to-the-zeitgeist kinda guy that getting off on the latest Pavement or Snoop Doggy Dogg or whoever in no way diminishes or invalidates your undying affection for *Stranded* or *Don't Stand Me Down* or *Barry White: The Collection* or the live version of Bowie's 'Heroes' by Blondie, the B-side of 'Atomic'. You realise that the death of Kurt Cobain is something of a landmark, but it means very little to you, and while you feel just dandy at a gig you feel fidgety and awkward at anything resembling a rave. You are not as truly young as, say, a friend of yours, who is nineteen, studies Goethe and Böll, and gets into arguments on the tube about who is cuter, Take That or East 17. She thinks Take That. She recommends a Bulgakov novel to you.

When Deborah Harry comperes 'A Night with the Velvet Underground' on Channel 4, you forget to tape it. It's not a statement. You've just got other things to do. Your name isn't Dagwood. The *Debravation* album is not a problem, and on 'Top Of The Pops', which doesn't cost you any biscuits to watch, she still exudes charisma, playing with the age factor as if it were an extra veil. There's something about the repackaging of old hits on B-sides, the remixes and rehashes and 'tribute' bands, which leaves you cold. Well, it's a different era, isn't it? Her influence pervades half the fashionable groups of the year. You catch her shows intermittently now. One involved whips and chains and you thought it shudderinducingly naff and out of touch.

Madonna simply doesn't cut it for you. She's the kind of thug-bloke you find repulsive, like Gazza. When militant feminist separatists try to usurp the music press, you are bemused by their selective amnesia. It's like Debbie Harry never happened.

❖

Sometimes you wish you could find *deepforeverlove*, but so far, in real life, there are only glimmers. Perhaps you just have to love yourself – the greatest, as they say, love of all. Well, that's never been a major problem. The more you learn about women the less you know. There are only three consistencies you can count on. All girls tie wispy, multi-coloured, transparent scarves to mirrors. All girls witter on unceasingly about their mothers. All girls, however robust, possess skinny, tiny wrists that effortlessly break your heart.

Otherwise, they're snowflakes with attitude.

❖

The last time you *saw* Deborah Harry was at The Labatts Apollo. When you were younger this had a less preposterous name (Hammersmith Odeon) and a New Year's Eve TV special from here featured Blondie. It filled you with adrenaline. Through the cathode rays came forth . . . dynamite. This time, you go, in the flesh, with someone who has just taught you to juggle, and who, seeing your flat for the first time that day, has expressed her dismay with words like 'pigsty', 'lazy', and 'men'. In all candour you'd rather spend the evening in your pigsty being lazy with her than go traipsing off to some pop concert, but you loyally feel you must make the pilgrimage, you cannot lapse, not you. You find the tickets, find your coats, and off the two of you go. A month later you will be in Paris with this highly vocal and unrestrained woman and when an advert coos 'toute feu, toute femme', she will add the coda 'toute bollocks'.

So you're in the hall, and Debbie Harry and Chris Stein and their latest band are working hard to stir some warmth from a lacklustre audience, and the seating plans are irksome, and there's no bar and no smoking, and everyone there is older (conjecture) and staider (fact) than you two. You want to support The Queen of Pop or principle, of course you do, but this extraordinary girl, a somewhat more tangible concept, is wiggling her backside close to you, and whenever you talk to each other the dorks in the next seats frown disapprovingly.

Basically you're not relaxed and this isn't Paradise. So you surprise yourself.

'Let's go for a drink and chat', you say. 'No, really. That's what I'd like to do.'

'Whatever', she shrugs. You walk the gauntlet of glances

from the front to the back of the hall. Deserters. Traitors.

Ladies and gentlemen, you have left the building. You head for a riverside pub.

'Are you sure about this?' she says with concern. She doesn't pretend to understand your previous obsession, but she's heard you mention it. She's seen you shake your head with mild embarrassment while doing so, as if to suggest you're a wiser, more self-possessed adult nowadays.

'I'm sure. I didn't feel right. In there. With you.'

'We can always go back if you want.' Her hair is black and purple and you are gazing at it both admiringly and absently.

'No . . .' You're trying to find your cigarettes in your pocket. 'I like you. You're, like, a real woman.'

'I *am* a real woman, cretin.'

'Granted. Come on, I could murder a pint.'

◇

Before you start writing this thing you root out all your old memorabilia, your Blondie records and books and posters, other impetuous acquisitions from the past. You have a lot of fun. You pick up *Making Tracks* for a browse and something falls to the floor from between pages 82 and 83. It's leaves. Pressed green leaves. Stuck squidgily to the pages is what must once have been a red rose. It's yellowy-brown with fuzzy-white patches. It's seen better days. But it's still there.

So *that's* where it was.

THE FALL

...TO ANY OF THE CLAUSES OR TERMS CONTAINED HEREIN HAS
...NDING AND SERVES NO CONSTRUCTIVE PURPOSES UNLESS FIRST   DH.
...ARTISTS MANAGEMENT AND ANY SUCH ALTERATION THEN MADE
...LLED BY BOTH PARTIES.

...AINS THE RIGHT TO APPROVE ALL SUPPORT ACTS AND (IF ANY)
...TO THE BILL.

...UNDERSTOOD THAT NO CANS OR BOTTLES ARE TO BE
...AUDITORIUM.

...F THE ARTIST   SOD-OFF

...HE PROMOTER   Dawn Holliday

                                   'DAWN'
                                   HOLLIDAY

THE FALL

MERCHANDISING DEAL
80% TO ARTISTS 20% TO SLIM'S
ARTIST PROVIDES SELLER

26. **PASSES**
UNDER NO CIRCUMSTANCES CAN THE PROMOTER ISSUE PHOTO PASSES WITHOUT
THE PERMISSION OF THE ARTISTS TOUR MANAGER. IF THE PROMOTER HAS ANY
V.I.P. GUEST THEN A HOSPITALITY SUIT MUST BE PROVIDED AT THE
PROMOTERS EXPENSE, AWAY FROM THE WORKING AREAS AND THE BACKSTAGE AREA.

                                         20% to Slim's

27. **MERCHANDISING**
THE ARTISTS SHALL HAVE THE ABSOLUTE RIGHT TO SELL VARIOUS MERCHANDISING
ITEMS AT A SUITABLE PLACE WITHIN THE VENUE. IT IS FURTHER AGREED THAT
THERE SHALL BE NO COMMISSION UPON THE SALES OF THESE ITEMS DUE TO THE
PROMOTER. IT IS AGREED THAT OUTSIDE MERCHANDISE ...RS WITHOUT BE
ADMITTED INSIDE THE VENUE. ALL REASONABLE STE... ...KEN TO
PREVENT 'PIRATE' (UNLICENSED) MERCHANDISERS ...   ...VENUE
WHERE THE ARTIST IS TO PERFORM.

28. **MIXING CONTROL BOARDS**
THE PROMOTER AGREES TO MAKE PROVISION FOR ...
MORE THAN 75 FEET (25 M) FROM THE FRONT O...
AUDITORIUM (STALLS) FOR THE ARTISTS' SCRA...
THIS AREA MUST NOT BE UNDER A BALCONY ...
TO THE ARTISTS PERSONNEL, BUT SECURED FR...

29. **SOUND CHECK/CHANGE OVER**
THE ARTIST SHALL HAVE THE FIRST RIGHT ...
PROPERTIES USED IN THE PRODUCTION. A...
AND PROPERTIES SHALL NOT BE MOVED, ...
OTHER THAN THE ARTISTS PERSONNEL WI...
ARTISTS TOUR MANAGER. THERE SHALL ...
EACH PERFORMANCE FOR THE CHECKING ...
...AND EQUIPMENT BY THE ...

THE FALL

7. **SECURITY**

A) THE PROMOTER SHALL AT HIS OWN EXPENSE EMPLOY AN ADEQUATE NUMBER OF SECURITY
GUARDS WHO SHALL PROTECT THE ARTIST, HIS BAND AND AUXILLIARY PERSONNEL AND
THEIR PROPERTY PRIOR TO, DURING AND AFTER THE PERFORMANCE. SECURITY
MUST BE PROVIDED IN THE AREAS OF THE DRESSING ROOMS AND STAGE. PARTICULARLY,
SECURITY PROTECTION SHALL COMMENCE UPON ARRIVAL OF THE ARTISTS EQUIPMENT
AT THE VENUE.

...RITY MAN TO GUARD THE BANDS EQUIPMENT DH
...EN 2½ TO 3 OVERNIGHT.

...THE STAGE OR THE BACKSTAGE AREA UNLESS
...E PERFORMANCE AND PERMISSION HAS BEEN
...GER AND THEY ARE WEARING THE CORRECT

...ION TO GIVE ANY INTERVIEWS TO RADIO
...DURING THE TERM OF THIS CONTRACT.
...TIST HAS BEEN OBTAINED.

...UNLESS PRIOR AGREEMENT IS REACHED
...OVIDED.

...EL. THIS CONTRACT WITHOUT LIABILITY
..., RIOT OR CIVIL DISORDER MAY
...LVES (THE ARTIST) OR THEIR CREW.

...OR OTHER ADVERTISING MATERIAL.
...ORMANCE, NOT SHALL THE ARTISTS
...Y ANY PRODUCT OR COMPANY, UNLESS
...STS MANAGEMENT.

...STS ACT IS BEING PAID ON   11 UE 05 approved. DH
...UPPLY:

...THER THAN TWO DAYS BEFORE THE
...ING FORTH THE NUMBER OF TICKETS
...SHALL BE SOLD ACCORDINGLY WITH

...HALL BE PAID TO THE
...IST TO THE RELEVANT

THE FALL

SAN FRANCISCO HIPPY RIDER

C) THE PROMOTER AGREES IF HE CANNOT SUPPLY CLAUSE (A) AND (B) THEN AT NO
COST TO THE ARTIST HE WILL SUPPLY TWO DAY ROOMS IN A NEARBY GOOD QUALITY
HOTEL. TO BE DISCUSSED WITH THE TOUR MANAGER A MINIMUM OF TEN DATE PRIOR
TO THE DATE OF PERFORMANCE.

                     1993
                     4-5 - SEP 1991

NOTE: (A) IF NO KIT IS AVAILABLE THE PROMOTER AGREES TO PROVIDE ADEQUATE
SECURITY PERSONNEL TO PROTECT THE ARTIST, THE ARTIST MANAGEMENT/CREW'S
POSSESSIONS IN THE DRESSING ROOM, DURING THE ENGAGEMENT.

NOTE: (B) IF THERE ARE NO HOT SHOWER OR BATH FACILITIES AT THE VENUE, THEN
EVERY EFFORT SHOULD BE MADE TO PROVIDE WASHING FACILITIES THAT ARE CLEAN
AND AVAILABLE TO THE CREW.

                     SLIM'S S.F

6) **CATERING**
TO BE AVAILABLE ON ARRIVAL OF THE ARTIST AT THE VENUE:

48 LARGE CANS OF LAGER (HOLSTEN PILSNER) ~~...~~
4 LITRES ORANGE JUICE
4 LITRES APPLE JUICE
~~...~~
6 LITRES STILL WATER
~~...~~
~~20 BOTTLES OF MORE CHARNON CHAMPAGNE~~
~~2 BOTTLES GOOD WHITE WINE~~   no cigarettes ← !!
~~60 BENSON AND HEDGES CIGARETTES~~

A SELECTION OF BREAD, FRUIT, MEATS, CHEESES, ~~SWEETS, TEA AND COFFEE TO BE~~
AVAILABLE ALL DAY.

ALL THE ABOVE MUST BE PRESENTED IN THE CORRECT FASHION, WITH TABLE CLOTHS
METAL CUTLERY, GLASSES, BOTTLES OPENERS, SALT, PEPPER, REAL PLATES & CUPS,
E.T.C.

FRESH ICE MUST BE SUPPLIED.   hot meal after sound check.

WHERE THE ARTIST IS NOT SUPPLYING THEIR OWN CATERING, THE PROMOTER MUST
SUPPLY THE FOLLOWING:

A HOT MEAL FOR TEN PEOPLE AT A GOOD RESTAURANT (PLEASE UNDERSTAND THAT
THERE IS A VEGETARIAN IN THE FALL), NO TAKE AWAYS WILL BE ACCEPTED. THE
TIME OF THE MEAL WILL BE DISCUSSED WITH THE TOUR MANAGER.

COFFEE AND TEA AND SOFT DRINKS TO BE AVAILABLE FROM LOAD IN, ALL DAY,
FOR THE CREW, ALONG WITH 24 CANS OF BEER AFTER SOUNDCHECK.

GOOD HOT MEALS TO BE PROVIDED FOR THE CREW (10 PEOPLE) (3) M.E.S

ON SOME OCCASIONS THE ARTIST IS MORE THAN HAPPY TO PROVIDE THEIR OWN

to: MR. CHRIS ROBERTS
    LONDON W4

FROM: MARK E. SMITH
      'THE HOUSE OF CONTEMPT'
      MANCHESTER M25
      CHICAGO SUB-STATE

      DECEMBER 1993

SUBJECT :   MUSICAL INFLUENCE IN GREAT BRITAIN on BIG-HEAD HERE

"You and I HAVE SEEN TREES GROW...This is our heart's desire,
for the work in Greater Manchester to grow even more.
We have seen growth during our two years here,but we are
praying for more workers from England to join the Ministry
and 'Branch Out' !
We praise the Lord for Mark Johnstone,from Liverpool."

                    QUOTE: 'JIM & JAN'S JOYOUS JOTTINGS'
                           M/CR FLYER DEC. 1993
                           (Child Evangelism Fellowship
                           (TM) INC.

1. TOO MANY POISON HEADS KNOCKING ABOUT.

        Apart from being an example of scouse/U.S. Insidious
infiltration of my home town,the above quote also illustrates
the appalling influence The Beatles have had on our popular
culture over the last 25 years.

        As a youth,music was a rare thing in my home,but surely
The Searchers were the only good Liverpool group ? This
was mainly because they never wrote any of their own songs,
but could arrangeimpeccably and showed marvelous intelligence
in choosing their covers,as Elvis did.

        THERE IS NO EXPANDING ON THE ABOVE AS I AM NOT A
        MATURE STUDENT.

        As a youth,I had no particular heroes music-wise,that's
why I formed a group in the first place.

        I n a way,popular music has turned us into a nation of
Fusspots,with the endless blatherings of people coming up
to their late 40's /and/or RETIREMENT AGE they don't
make them like that any more, or,perhaps worse,the second
hand sexuality of the 70's revivalists.

        The Kinks would not get a record contract nowadays,and
were virtually ignored "THEN".

                                                            129

~~

Therefore we are left with a barrel of stinking sweet molasses.
And the Vapoarisation of reality.

The British Music business is probably the last vestige of
British industry in it's incompetence and wilful self-destructive-
ness.I sometimes find that I adapt well to it because I spent
three years when I was a teenager working on Salford /Manchester
and Liverpool docks as they collapsed to become cinemas etc.-
you come across the same illiteracy in the management,the smugness
of the new boys in suits knowing they can do it, and the same working
class skivers cum workers (incl. me) coming through the gate every
day to prove them right.

I was going tow write this piece around the daftness of teen
music but that's a bastard assumption on my part-in 1976 society
and rock music was as rotten as it is now.

Fortunately,these bastards in Fun City eventually go to bed,
as I heard a car thief say the other day in a bar.

POISON NECKLACE ALERT

IST DAS TODTEN DANDY !

MARCH 1992.

3. Art crawl sponsored by Manchester Arts Council.
   This entails walking around what the Council think are so-called
   typical Manchester pubs with an entourage of arts critics from
   across the U.K.,all important,but I NOTICED NOBODY from 'Frieze'
   or Italy was present. In each bar there is an artists' work.The
   start off line is snipped by Tony Wilson. We,with me as second guide
   have to traipse round these so-called pubs full of Manchester United
   reserves and Granada t.v. extras.Wilson,atypical,disappears.

   I talk to the major newspapers' art critics,and am amazed to
   discover for instance that they know little of Tinterreto,Titian,
   and when I mention Wyndham Lewis I am accused of being a Fascist. I r
   I refuse all free drinks,look round at about 10.15 p.m. and every body
   is gone.

4. -11.30.a.m. Gear pick-up from rehearsal place.

5. My birthday

6. Studio in Rochdale

until; 14th.
            concert SWANSEA
               then into NOTTS./LEICES/STAFFS/MCR
            writ notes to myself;
          DO NOT GO ROUND EXPLAINING YOURSELF

PART THRREE _ (IDOL WORHIP)

PRISON SERIAL KLLR CUTURE AND WHAT DOE IT HAVE TO DO WITH THE PERFORMING RIGHTS SOCIETY LTD ?

xx

(A) General Overview 1994

Soungarden,the group is murmured.As with Therapy? and the Seattle groups there is a pathetic,polytechnic class obsession with crims, Manson et.al.I find this culturally TODT,musically moribund and Check shirt bound.

SCENE: A 28-29 year old mature student in a young girlś flat:

    "HEŚS Slightly too old,perhaps , for the body-pierced/pseudo-

    Satanic look. HE adopts,instead, a fresh faced,suede clad almost clean ,educated soccer player kakk image.We should not embrace this as it now makes him more difficult to spot.

    This anally-retented crusty through his young 'friends'(girl) rcord collection does rifle. He comments on the pitiful lack of GRAM PARSONS,BIG STAR,CROSBY STILLS AND NASH records and her woeful ignorance
    ─────────── of more up-to-date groups like THE SMASHING PUMPKINS and THERAPY?(HIS greatest achievement so far is the inclusion of HIS name-misspelt- in the acknowledgement and Thank Yous to the Section of the Clynton Von Heylin Book Of Rock And Roll Writing.

    HE,to the amusement of people who work in record shops,refers to his Rock Heroes - JONI,KURT,PATTI - by their first names as if personal confidantes.

    He explains to his 'friend'(girl) his present collating of information on his birthday present from Dad word processor for the R.E.M. definitive biography."

    -This sort of thing goes on.HE must have been ten when "PATTI" came out.

SWITCH_____

B)   SCENE: L.p. PARTY TIME. MANCHESTER. LAUNCH circa early 1992.
        LOCATION: THE GRANADA TOURS TOR PLOT- The Mock Rovers' Return.
    UNNAMED GROUP.
    M.E.S. Notes; GRANADA TOUR. WHEN THE BOUNCERS LET ON TO YCU KNOW
                    THERE'S SOMETHING UP.
                    T.CHRISTIAN FROM THE T.V. IS TRYING TO BE YOUR PAL

                HE IS CROWING THAT HE CAN'T BE HERE TONIGHT,HE IS JAMAICA

    BOUND.   ////

part three 'IDOL WORSHIP' continued;

WHAT'S GONI the roadie from some Manchester group trying to prove ?
hear: 'THERE's STUDENTS SLEEPING ON AND IN THE STREETS AND CHURCHES

OF MANCHESTER'
    DO NOT DELEGATE ME AS YOUR BULLSHIT MARTYR.

back to the launch;

  Where are the instigators of this fiasco to be seen ?

Off to Jamaica ,no doubt. Or mumbling in some hotel or coach about
the ungratefulness of the rubbish group.

Then: Granada ,Boddingtons,the amiable bloke from Leeds,and that
thalidomide bloke troop in.

Then the crooksx who did the Olympic bid.
'Who is the promoter of this "gig"' I'm asked.
Overheard: 'By the way,why are you trying to put it on my account?"

The N.M.E. Grunges and COMPLIMENT;
Because, Smith;

You're the Joker in some free give-away playing card racket.

Get off it :
Get off off it :
Get right off it.

THE   END

BAR PART KEK FOUR,Overleaf.

Banana Republic: Memories of a Suburban Irish Childhood

Joseph O'Connor

IN THE SUMMER OF 1977 I was thirteen years old and pretty miserable with my life. My parents' marriage – unhappy for a long time – had finally disintegrated in the most acrimonious circumstances. My father had moved out of the house, applied to the courts for custody of myself, my two sisters and my brother, and won his case. On the day he had come back to collect us and take us to our new home, I had asked him to let me stay living with my mother. I felt sorry for her, I suppose, and I did not want her to be left on her own. My father agreed that I could do this. He was very good about it.

We lived in a five-bedroomed house in Glenageary, a middle-class suburb of Southside Dublin. There was a large stain on the gable wall, which, if you glanced at it in a certain light, looked like the map of Ireland. I always thought that meant something important, but I could never figure out what exactly. My parents, both of whom came from working-class Dublin backgrounds, had slogged and scraped hard to buy ᵥᵥ this house, at a time when things must have seemed full of possibility for them. They must have had great plans for what they would do in that house. But in the summer of 1977, with only myself and my mother living there now, the house seemed unutterably empty, haunted by lost expectations.

We fought a lot, my mother and I. She had wonderful qualities. She also had a passionate and mercurial nature, which the circumstances of her life had somehow forced down a wrong turn, so that it had taken the shape of anger. She possessed a capacity for doing great harm to people she loved, and that must have made her very unhappy. When I think about her now, I try to do so with compassion and love, because, like all unhappy people, she deserved that. But in those days, we hurt each other a lot, my mother and I. We didn't see eye to eye on *anything*. Sometimes she would throw me out of the house; other times I would simply walk out to get away from her. So what I'm saying is that I spent a good deal of the very hot summer of 1977 just wandering around the streets of Dublin, by myself.

And an odd thing was happening in Dublin in the summer of 1977. All of a sudden, a strange thing called punk rock had arrived in town. People were suddenly talking about it, everywhere you went. Up and down Grafton Street, in the arcades of the Dandelion Market on Saint Stephen's Green, in Freebird Records – a sleazily glamorous shop down on the quays of the river Liffey – the young people of my own age were all talking about punk rock.

At first in Dublin, punk rock was nothing much more than a feeling. I mean, nobody *knew* very much about it. It was said that it had been started over in London the year before, by a group called the Sex Pistols, who swore at people during interviews and were generally controversial. But nobody I knew had much more knowledge than that. Punk had been initially perceived as just another English invention, I suppose, another weird Limey oddity, in the same culturally wacko league as eel pie, pantomime dames and 'The Good Old Days'.

But that summer, posters for homegrown punk rock groups – or, more accurately, groups which masqueraded as punk groups – suddenly started to appear around Dublin. I remember starting to notice them, in places like The Coffee Inn on Anne Street, where I used to go and sit for hours over a single coca-cola. Posters for The Atrix, The Blades, The Boyscoutz, Big Self, Microdisney, Berlin, The New Versions, Rocky deValera and the Gravediggers, The Vultures, DC Nien, The Bogey Boys, The Radiators from Space. I may be wrong about some of these bands – I mean that I may have got their dates of birth wrong by a few months – but in my mind and memory, they all appeared in Dublin in the hot summer of 1977. I remember seeing the names of these new bands on these lurid posters, how exotic and mysterious the words seemed, how funny sometimes. There was a band called Free Booze, who had called themselves this because it was a good way to catch people's attention. And there was an odd little outfit of Northside born-again Christians, who played Peter Frampton songs, and who, it was said, would never amount to anything. In the summer of 1977, they were just about to change their name from The Hype to U2.

All these bands had sprung up more or less overnight in Dublin, it seemed to me. And at around the same time, a disc jockey called Dave Fanning, who worked on a pirate radio station called ARD, had started to play punk rock on his show.

Also, a strange new music magazine called *Hot Press* had just started up, carrying regular articles about punk rock, reviews of records, news of punk rock gigs. It was odd. But slowly, punk rock was starting to seep into Dublin. And in the summer after my brother and sisters went away to live with my Dad, I spent many nights in my room listening to Dave Fanning, reading Bill Graham or Niall Stokes in the *Hot Press*, avoiding my mother and wondering what to make of my life, and of punk rock.

It is important to say that this was a time when Dublin did not really exist on the world rock and roll map. We had Thin Lizzy and Rory Gallagher and a Celtic heavy metal band called Horslips, but that was about it. Foreign acts simply did not play in Ireland. It would have been almost unheard of for a big American or British band to gig in Dublin. The city had no pop culture. But in the summer of 1977, when I was thirteen, into this vacuum stepped a monstrous and slavering spirit.

Punk had a notion of secrecy about it in Ireland, a vague redolence of semi-illegality. Someone once told me that when Freebird Records first got in copies of the Sex Pistols record *Never Mind the Bollocks*, for instance, the customs officers had obliterated the word 'Bollocks' with strips of red sellotape. And RTE, the national radio station, refused to play punk at all. 'Punk rock is junk rock' announced Larry Gogan, then Ireland's foremost disc jockey. Punk felt kind of taboo. So to people of my age, it felt attractive.

I got a job that July, working as a teaboy on a building site in Dalkey, which was near where I lived with my mother. It was great to get out of the house, wonderful to have somewhere to go during the days. One of the labourers on the site was a tall, scrawny fellow called Hubert. Hubert was about nineteen, I suppose, from the working-class suburb of Sallynoggin. His language was atrocious. He peppered his sentences with the word 'fuck'; sometimes he would even insert it between the syllables of another word. One day, for instance, I heard him refer to his home town as Sallyfuckin-Noggin.

Hubert had worked as a bus conductor for a time, before being dismissed in mysterious circumstances and coming to lift blocks on the sites. There were two things which made his life complete. The first was pornography. He had a vast and comprehensive collection of *Playboys* and *Penthouses*, which had been sent over every month for some years by his brother in England. (Such publications are not legally available in Ireland.) Hubert would cut pictures out of these magazines and sell them individually to the other men on the site, thus garnering enormous profits. It was fifty pence for a picture which featured a pair of breasts, I remember, and seventy-five pence for what Hubert called 'a gee' – a coarse Dublin euphemism for a vagina. 'Seventyfuckinfive pence a gee-shot', he would sigh, shaking his head and absolutely refusing to haggle.

The second thing that made Hubert's life complete was punk rock. He loved it. He absolutely adored it, and he would talk to me about it for hours at a time, while we were supposed to be working. He told me about an establishment in town called Moran's Hotel, in the basement of which there were punk rock concerts almost every night. Hubert seemed to know a lot about punk rock. It was all about being 'against society', he said, it was about 'smashing the system'. He himself was 'against society', he assured me fervently. There were legions of people in the basement of Moran's Hotel every night of the week who were also 'against society', and they had stuck safety pins through their ears, cheeks and noses to prove it.

The bands who played in Moran's Hotel were against society too, all of them. But the worst of the lot, Hubert confided, the mankiest shower of louse-ridden, no-good, low-down bowsies ever to plug in a Marshall, ram up the volume and hammer out a three-chord trick, was a band called the Boomtown Rats. They were 'fuckin' scum', Hubert would say, and he would smile in a fondly contented way when he said this, as though attaining the state of fuckin' scumhood was a development in which a person would take considerable pride. 'They don't even fuckin' wash themselves', he would beam, although, how he was in a position to know such a thing was always kept secret.

I would have loved to go to Moran's Hotel, of course, but being under-age, I couldn't. Yet I was frantically curious about this crowd of licentious and festering reprobates, the Boomtown Rats. I wondered what they would be like. The only live act I had ever seen before was Gary Glitter, performing in a television studio at RTE. I wondered if these Boomtown Rats could possibly be as entertaining as Gary. One day Hubert told me that I would soon have a chance to find out. The Boomtown Rats had been booked to play a big outdoor show in Dalymount Park soccer ground. And there must have been a bit of a run on gee-shots that week, because Hubert had bought me a ticket as a present.

That August afternoon, having lied to my mother about my destination – I think I said I was going to a boy scouts' day out – I went to the concert with Hubert and his girlfriend Mona. Mona was a healthy-looking girl, with the arms of a docker and a bewildering vocabulary of swear words. It was a very hot day and the stadium was packed full of people. Thin Lizzy and Fairport Convention were headlining the concert, but I did not care about that, mainly because Hubert had said these bands were not sufficiently 'against society'. So, like him and Mona, I only cared about the Boomtown Rats. When their arrival was announced over the PA, I thought Hubert was going to ascend body and soul into heaven, Virgin Mary-wise, so screechingly enthusiastic did he become.

I had never experienced anything quite like the phenomenal excitement as the band sloped onto the stage, picked up their instruments and began to play. I felt as though a lightning storm was flickering through my nerve endings. It's something you never really forget, the first time you hear the scream of an electric guitar, the thud of a bass or the clash of a real hi-hat cymbal. The lead singer, Bob Geldof, looked like an emaciated and drooling Beelzebub, as he leapt and tottered around the boards, spitting out lyrics into his microphone. The keyboard player, Johnny 'Fingers' Moylett, wore pyjamas on stage, an act of the most unspeakable and unprecedented sartorial anarchy. The bassist, Pete Briquette, lurched up and down leering dementedly, as though suffering from a particularly unpleasant strain of bovine spongiform encephalopathy. And if guitarists Gerry Cott and Gary Roberts, and drummer Simon Crowe, looked relatively normal, you still would have had considerable reservations about the prospect of any one of them babysitting your sister.

They played their music frantic and fast, incredibly LOUD, with a curious mixture of passion, commitment and utter disdain for the audience. I loved them. I had never heard a noise like this in my life. I was nailed to the ground by it. When they thrashed into their first single 'Looking After Number One', I swear to you, every single hair on my body stood up.

Don't give me love thy neighbour
Don't give me charity
Don't give me peace and love from your good lord above
You're always gettin' in my way with your stupid ideas
I don't want to be like you.
I don't want to be like you
I don't want to be like you
I'm gonna be like ME!

Now, this was what I called music. I went home that night with my head pounding and my heart reeling. My mother was waiting, of course, and she spent several hours yelling at me, which made my headache even worse. But I felt empowered by the music, I really did. It sounds so naïve now, I know, but that's the way it was. I felt that I had witnessed a kind of revelation. I felt that life was actually very simple. All you had to do, if someone was getting on your case, was tell them to fuck away off, that you didn't want to be like *them*, that you wanted to be like YOU! I told my mother this and she didn't exactly see things my way, to put it mildly. But it was the summer of 1977, you see. It all seemed very simple.

Back in school, in September, I told my friends all about the Boomtown Rats. I had five friends, Andrew McKimm, Andrew Deignan, Nicky, Conor and John. I think we were friends because nobody else liked us. Also, John's parents were separated, like my own, and Conor's mother had died, as had Andrew Deignan's father. So we felt we had something in common, in some odd way. I think we felt we had experienced more interesting pain than other people, although, of course, being teenage boys, we didn't talk much about such things. It turned out that Conor, a shy and very good-looking fellow, had heard about the Boomtown Rats himself. He had read an article about them – he was the one of our group who used to read articles – and it transpired that several members of the band, Bob Geldof and Johnny Fingers included, had actually *been to our school*.

If I had been interested in the Rats before, my enthusiasm rocketed through the roof now. These leprous anti-establishment scumbags had actually been to *my school*. Blackrock College, the alma mater of Irish President Eamon de Valera, this priest-run joint that had always been famous for taking in the carbuncular and prepubescent sons of the Dublin middle class and churning out obedient wageslaves had somehow produced the Boomtown Rats! How had this possibly happened? There was hope for us all, it seemed.

Now, there is a television programme in Ireland called 'The Late Late Show'. Its genial host, Gay Byrne, is a middle-aged man of polite manners and conservative views. It is often jokingly said in Ireland that Gaybo is the most powerful man in the country, and, like many jokes in Ireland – as opposed to Irish jokes – it contains the seed of a profound truth. One evening that autumn, Bob Geldof and the Rats were booked to appear on 'The Late Late Show'. Once again, I lied to my mother, so that I could get out of the house and go up to my friend's house to watch this.

The atmosphere in my friend's living room was electric, as we uncapped the shandy bottles, passed around the solitary spit-soaked cigarette, and waited for the messiah to descend.

Bob shambled onto the screen like an evil, bedraggled wino and sneered his way through the interview, in a furtive South-side drawl. He detested many things about Ireland, he said. He loathed the Catholic Church, he hated the priests who had taught him in Blackrock College, he disliked his father. He had only gotten into rock and roll in order to get drunk and get laid. Almost everything he said was greeted with horrified gasps and massed tongue-clickings from the audience, and wild cheers from myself and my friends. When the interview was over, the rest of the band came on and performed 'Mary of the Fourth Form', a feverish song about the seduction of a schoolteacher by a female student. As the number climaxed in a clamour of drums and wailing feedback, the studio audience was absolutely stunned.

'Well done, Bob,' smiled Gaybo, ever the professional. Geldof turned around, scowling, wiping the saliva from his lips with the back of his hand. 'Yeah, well if you liked it so much,' he snapped, 'just go and buy the record.' Fuck! The guy was giving cheek to Gay Byrne now! Well, this was something new and dangerous. This was practically revolution.

In Ireland, in the late nineteen seventies, this was absolutely astounding talk. This was the decade when one million people – a third of the entire population of the state – had attended a mass said by the Pope in Dublin's Phoenix Park. This was many years before Mary Robinson, or the divorce debate, or the legalisation of gay rights in Ireland. You could not legally buy a condom in Ireland in the late nineteen seventies, never mind go on the television and talk so blithely about getting drunk and getting laid and hating priests and disliking your father. And although I liked my own father quite a lot, Geldof's pungent cocktail of motormouth arrogance, unwise trousers and disrespect for authority really did appeal to me. In time, I couldn't get enough of it.

Soon after 'The Late Late Show', my friend Conor got a copy of the Boomtown Rats' first record and he taped it for me. It wasn't really punk at all, in fact, it was just souped-up rhythm and blues played with a lot of aggression. But there were some fantastic songs on it. 'Never Bite the Hand That Feeds' and 'Neon Heart', for instance. The music was raw, brimming with verve and a crisp visceral energy. But there were other things I admired about it. The songs were full of characters. I liked that. It made the songs seem like they were about real people. And there was a surprising facility for language, a gutsy pared-down approach to story-telling.

Sooner or later, the dawn came breaking
The joint was jumping and the walls were shaking
When Joey sneaked in the back door way
Pretending he was with the band, he never used to pay
He used to know all the people and know all the tricks
Used to lie up against the wall like he holding up the bricks.

But on the Boomtown Rats' first record there was also a slow piano-based ballad called 'I Can Make It If You Can'. It was a tender song of vulnerability and longing. I kept the tape beside my bed, and I would put on 'I Can Make It If You Can' every morning as soon as I woke up. I felt that this was the voice of a survivor, a guy who knew about pain. I felt he was singing to me, and to people like me, and that there was an integrity to what he was singing about. I played the tape until it wore out and couldn't be played any more. And there were many mornings around that time, I don't mind saying it, when that song really helped me to get out of bed. I can make it if you can.

The thing is, I used to get very down in those days. It began as pretty typical adolescent stuff but it got steadily worse, until it got very serious indeed, until it became real depression. I missed my brother and my two sisters. I missed my father more than I can say, and I wasn't getting on at all well with my mother. I was supposed to go and see my father every weekend, but my mother had gotten to the stage where she would simply not let me do this. She had begun to drink too much. She was also taking drugs, sleeping pills and tranquillisers. She was suffering from some dreadful pain, the poor woman, but at the time, I must say, I only cared about the suffering she was inflicting on me. Her temper became ferocious and unpredictable. She began to try hard to turn me against my father, and against my brother and sisters. She would insist that I was not to go and see my Dad, and I would not, most of the time, because I wanted a quiet life. And often when we did meet – he won't mind me saying it – my father and I had to meet in secret. A father and son, having to meet in secret. It's a shame things had to be like that.

I was so full of fear in those days that I would often feel fear clenched up inside me, like a fist, literally, like a physical thing. My life sometimes felt meaningless. In time, it actually got so I could see no future at all for myself. It is a terrible thing to feel so hopeless when you're so young, but I did for a while, and I have to tell you that honestly.

No teacher, no priest, no neighbour ever lifted a finger to help my family. There were three things, and three things only, which kept me going throughout those years. One was the love of my father, which was constantly and unselfishly

given. He never abandoned me, despite what he was going
through himself. The second was the support of my brother
and my sisters and my friends. And the third was Bob Geldof.

I would listen to his song 'I Can Make It If You Can', and
I would believe it. I simply felt that I could make it if Bob
Geldof could. I was naive enough to think that, but I'm grateful now for the naivety of youth. I associated myself with Bob
Geldof. He became a paradigm of survival, toughness and
courage. He would never *ever* get ground down by anything,
I felt, and thus, if I remembered that, neither would I. As
time went on, I began to think more about Bob Geldof. It
was the only thing I could do. I derived an active *personal*
pleasure from everything the Boomtown Rats got up to. I
bought everything they released – 'She's So Modern', 'Like
Clockwork', then the album *A Tonic for the Troops*. I really
did think their success had something to do with me. I felt I
was involved in it, inextricably linked to it, bound up with it
in ways that nobody but I could understand. I felt they were
singing to me. I thought of them as my friends, even though
I had never met them. Isn't that funny.

In November 1978, anyway, the Boomtown Rats became the
first ever Irish group to get to the top of the British charts. On
'Top of the Pops' that week, as he jabbered the words of 'Rat
Trap' into his mike, Geldof shredded up a poster of Olivia
Newton John and John Travolta, whose twee single 'Summer
Nights' the Rats had just ousted from the number one slot. In
school, my friends and myself were speechless with joy. Conor
cut a photograph of Geldof out of the *Hot Press* and we stuck
it up in the Hall of Fame, where the framed images of all the
famous past pupils of the school had been hung. We stuck Bob
up there, among the bishops and diplomats and politicians who

had founded the state in which we lived. His gawky, snot-nosed face fitted exactly over a photograph of President de Valera, and this fact had the kind of exotically cheap symbolism which appeals very greatly to fourteen year-olds. It felt like a victory of sorts at the time, and if I am honest, it still does.

Soon after that, things in the life of my family began to worsen again. My mother took my father to court and some-how won back custody of my two sisters and my brother. It was an amazingly stupid decision by the courts, but in holy Catholic Ireland, bizarre legal opinion too often takes prece-dence over the rights of terrified children, or it did then, at any rate. Things went from bad to worse in the house. There were constant rows, terrible arguments. Our Dad was rou-tinely and absolutely denied access to us, and nobody official ever did a thing to help him. And there was fear. We experi-enced terror, the four of us children. We never knew from one moment to the next how my mother would behave towards us. There were many times when she treated us well – with affec-tion and love. But there were other times when she seemed to see us as enemies, and at those times, the atmosphere in the house was close to unbearable. I don't know how we got through it. I sure as hell couldn't do it now.

I listened to the Boomtown Rats all the time. I would listen to them for hours on end, and let them send me into a kind of comforting trance. 'I Don't Like Mondays', 'Diamond Smiles', I knew the words of their songs off by heart. I would recite them, over and over again in my head, over and over. There were many nights when I went to sleep with the words of 'I Don't Like Mondays' rattling around in my head, many mornings when I woke up still silently reciting them, like a prayer.

In December 1979, the Boomtown Rats came back to

Ireland. They were supposed to play a big concert in a marquee in Leixlip, but they had been denied permission by the authorities at the last minute. The Boomtown Rats were seen as dangerous and anti-establishment in Ireland, such was the murderous innocence of the times. The band took the authorities to court, and lost. That Christmas, my parents were back in court too. I went along with my mother, but the judge told me to leave. When I came out of the court and into the huge circular hall of the Four Courts building in Dublin I was upset and crying. An odd thing happened, then. Fachtna O'Ceallaigh, the Boomtown Rats' manager, was standing on the other side of the hall with his lawyers. I recognised him from the newspapers. His case was on at the same time as my parents' case. He was just standing there with his hands in his pockets, looking cool as fuck. He might have been wearing sunglasses, although I'm not sure. But I was very glad to see him standing there. I felt it was a good omen. It made me think of Bob.

Christmas was dreadful that year. Terrible. The atmosphere in the house was one of pure fear. Early in the new year the Rats released – unleashed would be a better word – the single 'Banana Republic', which deftly summed up their feelings about Ireland. By now, they were feelings which coincided greatly with my own.

> *Banana Republic, septic isle*
> *Suffer in the screaming sea*
> *Sounds like die, die, die*
> *Everywhere I go now*
> *And everywhere I see*
> *The black and blue uniforms*
> *Police and priests*

It was a devastating attack on a society whose achievements in posturing cant and hypocrisy had so far outstripped its achievements in morality. It was delivered with force and power, at a time when it needed to be so delivered. Nobody but Geldof would have had the guts to do it. I don't know how anyone else felt about it at the time, and I don't care. I admired Geldof for calling it the way he saw it. I still do admire him for that.

But it was to be the last big single for the Boomtown Rats. Not long after 'Banana Republic', things started to wane. There were rumours of drug-taking in and around the band, I don't really know if they were true or not. One way or the other, I think the Rats simply began to lose their way as the tastes of the record-buying public started to change. But I still chart where I was in those days, and what I was doing, by remembering their singles. 'Elephant's Graveyard' was January 1981, the month after my parents' last court case. 'Go Man Go' was August 1981, the month my mother had to go into hospital for a fortnight.

We never told my father about my mother's absence. Instead, we stayed in the house by ourselves and we went pretty wild, my brother, and my two sisters and I. We stayed up late, we drank, we painted the words FUCK THE POPE and BOOMTOWN RATS across the front doors of our garage. We were drunk with freedom. We practically trashed the house. We moved four mattresses into one room, and we slept there, with the door locked. That's the kind of dread we had. We left the Boomtown Rats on loud, almost all the time. That's what I remember now, the blankness in the eyes of my siblings, the intoxicating light-headedness of fear and freedom, the thud of the bass coming up through the floorboards, the nasal roar of Geldof's voice. When you are in trouble, it is odd where you find consolation.

When my mother came home from hospital, it was clear that things could never be the same again in the house. We had tasted something like liberation, and would not easily go back to being suppressed. One Sunday afternoon, three weeks after she came home, my two sisters ran away and returned to my father, where they were treated with the love, affection and respect they deserved. They never came back to Glenageary.

'Never in a Million Years' was released in November 1981, just after I started college. That month, things got too much for me at home and I moved out too. My father helped me to get a flat near college. I made some good friends in university but I wasn't happy. I had the habit of telling people bare-faced lies in those days, for pretty much no reason at all. I think it was something to do with our former existence at home. It had been an environment where lies had become the norm for survival, and where the truth was often to be feared. So I hurt some of the new friends I had made by carrying this bizarre approach to the notion of truth out into the real world. I also felt ripped apart with guilt and self-loathing for leaving my brother. I sometimes went to meet him in the afternoons – he attended a school just down the road from the campus – but, as had been the case with my father, we had to keep our meetings secret. One day, when I went to see him, he had brought along the copy of *Tonic for the Troops* which I had left in my mother's house on the day I had finally run away. That tore me to pieces, I don't know why.

'House of Fire' was released in February 1982, when I was

going out with a girl called Grace Porter. 'Charmed Lives' was June the same year, just after we broke up. 'Nothing Happened Today' was August 1982, just after I finished my first-year exams. Almost everything that happened to me in those days, I am able to mark with a song by the Boomtown Rats. They may not be the greatest records ever made, but they're memorable to me, because they were involved with my life, and with the things I was doing, and with the people I knew and cared about.

The single 'Drag Me Down' came out in May 1984. I remember this, because I bought it one cold afternoon in Dunlaoghaire Shopping Centre, before getting the bus up to Glenageary to visit my mother. She was surprised to see me, she seemed pleased at first. We talked for a while, although I don't recall much about what was said. I remember she asked me if I had a girlfriend now, and I said no, I didn't, for some reason, although in truth I did. I smoked a cigarette in front of her, and she was shocked that I was smoking. We had an argument, then, and we parted on bad terms. It was the last time I ever saw her. My mother died nine months later in a car crash. It was a Sunday morning. She was driving to Mass.

I went to Nicaragua that summer. I was utterly bewildered and confused about my mother's death. I couldn't really figure out what to feel about it, besides a grief of such depth that I couldn't understand it. I think I was probably a bit crazy, and longing to find some kind of frame into which I could fit the events of the last few years more clearly. So I ran away to Nicaragua to be by myself. I took a tape of the Boomtown Rats' last album, *In the Long Grass*; also, a tape of their last ever single, 'A Hold of Me'. In some ways I wanted to forget about home, and in other ways I wanted to remember every last thing.

But it's odd, the stuff that happens. One of the first people I met in Managua was Lyn Geldof, one of Ireland's leading journalists, and also, *inter alia*, Bob's sister. She's a terrific woman, very smart and bright and funny, and I was lucky enough to get to know her a little bit while I was there. Now, Bob had said some pretty critical things about his family life, but he hadn't ever spoken about Lyn much. I thought she was really lovely, and that Bob was very lucky to have a sister like that. I wondered if the things he had said about his family were all true, or if they had possibly been exaggerated, by the media, or even by Bob himself. I never asked Lyn about it, but it did often occur to me. Back in Ireland that summer, my own sister, Sinead, had decided to become a singer. She was about to leave for London, where Fachtna O'Ceallaigh – the Rats' old manager – was about to become *her* manager. I knew how talented she was, and that she would make it in music. What I didn't know about back then was her need to detonate regular explosions of lurid and sensational publicity. So I just didn't know how often that thought would occur to me again; the shockingly hurtful things that get publicly said about the families of pop stars.

That was the summer of Live Aid. Many people with left-wing views were uncomfortable with the idea of the project, and I was one of them, I have to admit. I felt that charity wasn't the best way to deal with the problems of the developing world. Maybe I was right, maybe I was wrong, I don't know any more. Like Woody Allen said, don't ask me why there were Nazis, I can't even get the can-opener to work. What I do know is that Geldof was clearly motivated by nothing but humanity, and that if those critics on the Left who took cheap shots at him had displayed something like the same humanity, both in their criticisms and in their politics, the world would be a better place.

I came back to Ireland and returned to college. Slowly, gradually, things began to calm down a bit in my life. But I often thought about the old days, and sometimes when I did, the Boomtown Rats would come into my mind. Their career seemed to have petered out by that stage. Geldof was probably the most famous person in the world, but the band hadn't made a record in a long time, and they seemed to have no plans to do so.

And then, in May 1986, amid rumours that the band was about to call it a day for good, they came back to Dublin to play at a charity event, featuring Van Morrison, U2, the Pogues, all the great and the good of the Irish rock world. The Rats played a stormer. They blew everyone away and received a tumultuous reception from the audience. After the main set, Geldof strolled up to the microphone for an encore. He seemed taken aback by the warmth of the crowd's affection. At first – unusually – he didn't seem to know what to say. He appeared a little lost as his eyes ranged over the crowd. 'Well, it's been a great ten years,' he muttered, then. 'So, rest in peace.'

The thundering drum roll began. The opening riff pounded out. The familiar chords, D, A, G, E. The last song the Boomtown Rats ever played in public was their first song, Geldof's hymn to snot-nosed anarchy and adolescent attitude, 'Looking After Number One'.

Don't give me love thy neighbour
Don't give me charity
Don't give me peace and love from your good lord above
I'M GONNA BE LIKE ME!!

It was at once a powerful homecoming, a stylishly ironic act of self-deprecation and a poignant farewell. And in some odd and quite profound sense, it seemed like a farewell to me too, a final goodbye to a time in my life that was over now. As I watched the show on television that day, I knew that I would leave Ireland again soon, that I would not come back for a long time, that I would try to forget about most of my past.

I came to England four months after that. I went to Oxford to do a doctorate, didn't like it much, dropped out. I came to London then, decided to stay there because I liked its anonymity, its vast size. All the things that other people hated about London, I loved. It was a great place in which to get lost, and that's what I did for a while, just kept to myself and got lost.

Gradually I lost touch with my old schoolfriends. I had ups and downs in my personal life, times of great joy too. I moved flat three or four times, and somewhere along the way I left behind all my old Boomtown Rats records. But I remember their force and power still, the healing power of their righteous indignation. And I suppose that sometimes the words don't seem quite as electrifying now as they did in Dalymount Park on a summer day when I was thirteen years old and breathless with discovery. But that doesn't bother me much. Because great pop music sometimes heals us in ways that we don't understand, or in ways that seem unbelievably trite or trivial when we look back. Great pop music is about the people who listen to it, and the circumstances in which they do so, and not really in the end about the people who make it. Maybe that's what's so great about it. I don't know.

A few years ago I wrote a novel called *Cowboys and Indians*, about the love of rock music, among other things. In the winter of 1991, after a reading I did in Dublin, a girl I used to know in the old days came up to me and said that my friend Conor, who had given me my first Boomtown Rats tape, was dead. Things hadn't worked out for him in Dublin, she said. He had left Ireland, like so many of the young people I knew. He had drifted around for a while, ended up in Paris, and been happy enough there. But then something bad had happened to him – she didn't know what exactly – and he had died.

I was so shocked. I could not believe what had happened. I had a lot to drink and I lay awake for hours, just thinking about the past, unrolling images from my childhood as though looking at a film. I cried a lot that night. When finally I fell asleep I dreamed about poor Conor. Sometimes – very occasionally – I dream about him still, and when I do, it's always the same happy dream. I see his laughing, shy face on the day we stuck the photograph of Bob Geldof up in the hall of fame in Blackrock College. I hear him whispering, 'Let's do it, Joe, come *on*, don't be afraid'. It's not the worst way to remember him. And I'm sure the Boomtown Rats are up on the wall in Blackrock College officially now. But we beat the authorities to it, me and my friend Conor. We beat them by a whole decade.

Last year, I was on a television programme in Ireland to talk about my novel, and Bob Geldof was one of the guests. I was extremely apprehensive about meeting him, because he had been such a hero of mine, and because he was connected

to so many painful memories, I suppose, and, also, because
I've met enough pop stars to know that they usually have the
intelligence quotient of a piece of toast. But he was absolutely
great. He had the air of a survivor. He seemed like a man
who had come through.

In the green room after the show, he introduced me to his
sister Cleo, and to his father. (He described his father as 'the
real Bob Geldof'.) He was very polite to everybody, he made
real efforts to include people in the conversation. We chatted
for a while about nothing at all, his eyes flitting around the
room as he talked, his hands running through his straggly hair.
When the time came to go I asked him if he wanted to come
out for a jar, but he said no. He was going out for a meal with
his family. So we shook hands and he got his stuff together
and sloped from the room with his father and his sister, a
guitar case under his arm. It was like watching a part of your
past walk out the door.

I never got the chance to tell him what was on my mind
that night. There were too many people around, and, anyway,
I suppose I hadn't really found the words I was looking for.
But when I think about it now, what I wanted to say was
actually very simple. It was this: when I was a scared kid, who
felt that there was little point to life, his music and his example
were second only to the love of my father and my stepmother
and my brother and sisters in keeping me going through all
the terror and misery. It helped me survive. It helped me sit
out the dark days, and wait for the better times to come.
And I don't care whether nobody likes the music now. Tastes
change, and times change, and so they should. Besides, a hell
of a lot of people didn't like it then. But *I* did. Big time. His
music embodied a worldview with which I felt I had some

connection. It opened my eyes to things that had never occurred to me before. Like the greatest pop music, it was fun, unpredictable, alive, iconoclastic, intelligent, witty, danceable, tender when it wanted to be, tough as nails when it had to be. It just made me feel better. It healed. And it made me think I could make it, if *he* could. A foolish and adolescent belief, if ever there was one. But in a world where I had to grow up too fast, at least Bob Geldof and his band allowed me to be foolish and adolescent just once in a while. I'm grateful indeed, for that little, or that much. I'm very grateful for that.